MARY FORD
NOVELTY CAKES

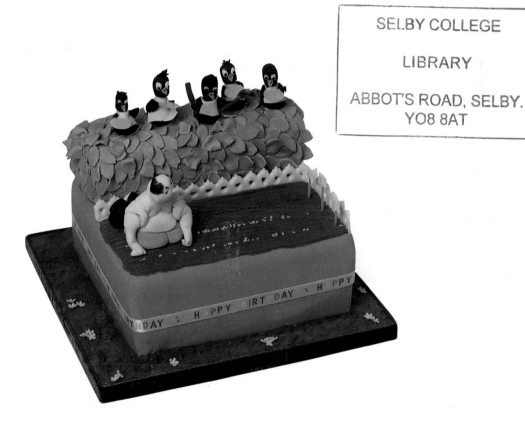

MARY FORD

A MARY FORD BOOK

Published 1996 by Mary Ford Publications Limited,
Emerson Court, Alderley Road, Wilmslow,
Cheshire SK9 1NX, England.

Typesetting by Russ Design & Production, Salisbury.

ISBN 0 946429 56 1

THE AUTHOR

Mary Ford is a leading name in UK cake decoration. She has inspired three generations of cake decorators through her cake artistry classes and her popular books are reaching an increasingly wide audience. Her titles have sold over 850,000 copies and Mary's classic 'Step-by-Step' method has been used in kitchens and classrooms around the world.

Mary is dedicated to passing on her craft. She takes great pride in ensuring that recipes and designs will work for beginners and accomplished cake decorators alike – so long as the instructions are followed. Creating new cakes is a great joy to her, but she is never too busy to answer a query or to talk to a former student.

She is helped in her work by her husband, Michael, the editorial director and photographer for all the books. Together they have created almost thirty titles in the last thirteen years.

ACKNOWLEDGEMENTS

Mary Ford acknowledges with grateful thanks the assistance of Mary Smith.

Mary Ford unreservedly recommends the use of Tate and Lyle Sugar.

Cakeboards Limited, 47-53 Dace Road, London E3 2NH. Manufacturers and suppliers for cake decorating equipment and decorations to the wholesale and retail trade.

CONTENTS

AUTHOR	3
INTRODUCTION	6
SUGAR	8
ALL-IN-ONE SPONGE CAKE	10
MADEIRA SPONGE CAKE	12
ALL-IN-ONE FRUIT CAKE	14
ALL-IN-ONE SWISS ROLL	16
ALMOND PASTE	18
BUTTER ICING	19
MODELLING PASTE	19
SUGARPASTE	20
ROYAL ICING	21
EQUIPMENT	22
HINTS AND TIPS	23
PORKY PIGLET	24
FISHING BOAT	26
RUGGER	29
BIRTHDAY ELEPHANT	29
BIG BREAKFAST	32
TOY SHOP	34
THE MUMMY	36
THE MAD HATTER	38
BIRTHDAY GALLEON	41
PUMPING IRON	44
FATHER'S DAY	46
ONE ARMED BANDIT	48
PESKY CROWS	50
STRAWBERRIES and CREAM	52
HEDGIE HEDGEHOG	54
HUMPTY DUMPTY	56
VINTAGE YEAR	58
3 TODAY	60
GOLF BAG	62
WINDMILL	64
PUSSYCATS	66

U.F.O.	68
PLUMMER'S MATE	70
CACTUS	72
CIRCUS TIME	74
SEWING BOX	77
FISH PLATTER	78
BILLIARDS	80
ALL AT SEA	82
RUCKSACK and BOOTS	84
HICKORY DICKORY DOCK	86
COUNT DRACULA	88
WEDDING TOPPERS	90
NOAH'S ARK	92
DUSTY BIN	96
CAKE BOXES	98
LUCKY HORSESHOE	100
FIREWORKS	102
BOW TIE and TAILS	104
SING-A-SONG OF SIXPENCE	106
FISHING CREEL	108
KING KONG	110
THE THREE LITTLE PIGS	112
CHRISTMAS GOODIES	115
CHRISTMAS CALLER	116
INDEX and GLOSSARY	118
MARY FORD TITLES	120

NOTE: WHEN MAKING ANY OF THE RECIPES IN THIS BOOK, FOLLOW ONE SET OF MEASUREMENTS ONLY AS THEY ARE NOT INTERCHANGEABLE.

INTRODUCTION

There is a great deal of pleasure to be had from cake decorating: the pleasure of creating a beautiful work of art, the joy of giving, and the pleasure of the recipient. I have always tried to share this pleasure with my readers.

But, as I am well aware, there is also an element of fun to be shared. The fun that comes from something a little different, a cake that brings a smile to the face, a design that makes you feel that bit brighter as you work. A cake that is unique and personal, that makes its recipient feel "This is specially for me."

Over the years, I have thoroughly enjoyed creating novelty cakes, whether they be for children or adults. With a little ingenuity and a touch of inspiration, it is possible to recreate old friends such as nursery rhymes or to create up to the minute favourites. A cake can be personalised, not just by a name but by creating an item that will really mean something to the recipient, linked perhaps to a hobby or special interest as well as the event. The possibilities are endless.

In this book you will find 45 new designs that assume no knowledge or experience of cake making and decorating. All you need is a steady hand and the ability to follow my step-by-step instructions. Every stage is carefully illustrated by colour photographs and concise directions.

These cakes will build up your decorating skills and expertise. However, if you are already an experienced decorator, you will find several cakes that bring out the best of your artistic skills, and there is the challenge of combining elements into an entirely new design of your own.

As usual, I have included recipes for basic cakes. The Madeira Sponge cuts well and is ideal for novelty cakes that need shaping. The cakes in this book are suitable for any occasion. They bring a new excitement to a birthday or other celebration. All are versatile. The Wedding Toppers are ideal for an informal wedding, but would not be out of place at a

formal gathering. On its own, the bride's hat can easily be transformed into an Easter bonnet. Simply add a daffodil or spring chicks. Count Dracula is ideal for a teenage birthday, but is equally suitable for young or old. He would feel at home on spooky Halloween, but could make a somewhat different declaration of love too.

I am often asked what are the secrets of cake artistry, I always respond that my many years of teaching cake design and decoration have taught me time, patience and practice are the cornerstones of success. Most of the designs in this book do not need icing skills and so you will not have to spend time on this beforehand. If you do need to practice an inscription, for instance, you can try it out on an upturned cake tin or any flat, clean surface. However, as colour is extremely difficult to remove from sugarpaste, you may need to practice painting or colouring a design or figure beforehand. Careful planning avoids mistakes and, if the worst does happen, the best thing is to cover it with a decoration. Do not try to hurry things. If you allow yourself plenty of time when modelling, you will find that appealing figures are easy to make with a minimum of skill.

Always read through all the stages before commencing work and gather together everything you will need. It is always worth making one or two extra delicate items just in case of breakages, and remember that it is virtually impossible to match coloured sugarpaste or icing, so make a slightly more than adequate batch for your needs.

I hope that you will have many happy hours creating the designs in this book.

Have fun!

Mary Ford

SUGAR

Sugar, an essential ingredient in the kitchen, originates in the giant grass-like sugar cane which grows in tropical climates such as the Caribbean, Mauritius and Fiji. It is a flavour enhancer, preservative and natural sweetener as well as contributing to the texture of food.

Sugar can aptly be described as 'a taste of sunshine' because it is manufactured in plants as a direct result of the sun's energy, through a process known as photosynthesis. However, whilst all plants make sugars, commercially produced sugars are extracted only from sugar cane and sugar beet.

The extraction process used by Tate & Lyle removes undesirable impurities and produces the characteristic crystalline structure without the addition of any artificial colourings, flavourings or preservatives.

Nutritionally brown and white sugars are virtually identical, but the distinctive colour and flavour of brown sugar arises from molasses, which is the syrup remaining after all the sugar has been removed from the cane juice. When manufacturing white sugar, the molasses is completely removed whilst the different brown sugars contain more, or less, of the syrup depending on the flavour and colour required.

Therefore, careful selection of the type of sugar used can greatly enhance the finished taste and texture.

Icing Sugar: The finest of all sugars. It dissolves rapidly and is especially used in making icings, smooth toppings, confectionery, meringues and cake frostings. Apart from decorating cakes, icing sugar is perfect for sweetening cold drinks and uncooked desserts, as its fine texture makes it easy to dissolve.

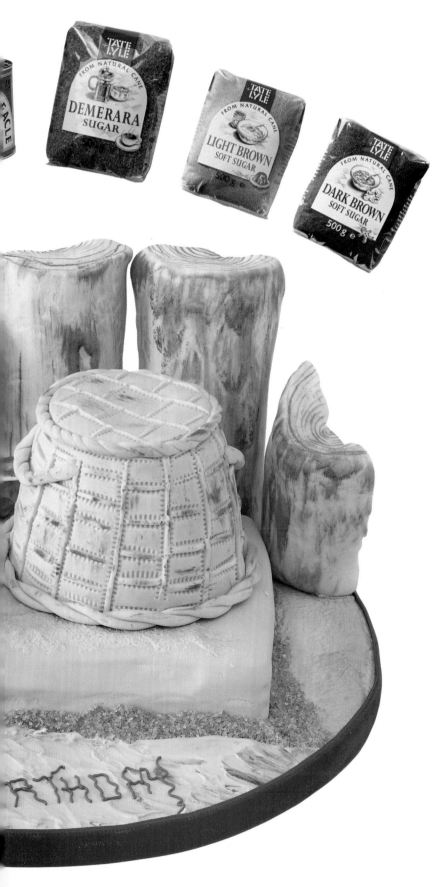

Granulated Sugar: Granulated sugar has a very pure crystal and is an ideal boiling sugar. It can be used for sweetening tea, coffee, sprinkling over cereals or frosting cakes and glasses for decoration.

Caster Sugar: Caster sugar is a free flowing sugar with very fine crystals. Excellent for use in baking cakes and other baked goods as the fine white grains ensure smooth blending and an even texture.

Lyle's Golden Syrup: Golden syrup is a partially inverted syrup produced from intermediate refinery sugar liquors when they are heated in the presence of an acid. It is an ideal sweetner and can be used in cooking and baking to add bulk, texture and taste.

Lyle's Black Treacle: Black treacle is a dark, viscous liquid with a characteristic flavour. It is obtained from cane molasses, a by product of sugar refining.

Demerara Sugar: This sugar has a golden colour with a unique flavour that makes it particularly popular in coffee. The grain is larger than granulated and is ideal for decorating biscuits and cakes, sprinkling over desserts and making crunchy toppings.

Light Brown Soft Sugar: This sugar is fine grained, creamy golden in colour and has a mild syrup flavour. It is best used when creamed with butter or margarine in any recipe that requires a deeper, richer colour and fuller flavour.

Dark Brown Soft Sugar: This sugar is darker with a strong flavour and is ideal for rich fruit cakes, gingerbread, spiced teabreads and puddings.

9

ALL-IN-ONE SPONGE CAKE

This sponge is ideal for birthday cakes and cutting into shapes for novelty cakes.

SPONGE TIN SHAPES	SPONGE TIN SIZES					
ROUND	15cm (6in)	18cm (7in)	20.5cm (8in)	23cm (9in)	25.5cm (10in)	28cm (11in)
SQUARE	12.5cm (5in)	15cm (6in)	18cm (7in)	20.5cm (8in)	23cm (9in)	25.5cm (10in)
PUDDING BASIN	450ml (¾pt)	600ml (1pt)	750ml (1¼pt)	900ml (1½pt)	1 litre (1¾pt)	1.2 Litre (2pt)
LOAF TIN		18.5 x 9 x 5cm 450g (1lb)			21.5 x 11 x 6cm 900g (2lb)	
Self-raising flour	45g (1½oz)	60g (2oz)	85g (3oz)	115g (4oz)	170g (6oz)	225g (8oz)
Baking powder	¼tsp	½tsp	¾tsp	1tsp	1½tsp	2tsp
Soft (tub) margarine	45g (1½oz)	60g (2oz)	85g (3oz)	115g (4oz)	170g (6oz)	225g (8oz)
Caster sugar	45g (1½oz)	60g (2oz)	85g (3oz)	115g (4oz)	170g (6oz)	225g (8oz)
Eggs	1 size 4	1 size 3	1 size 1	2 size 3	3 size 3	4 size 3
Baking temperature	------------------ 170°C (325°F) or Gas Mark 3 -------------------------------					
Approximate baking time	20 min	25 mins	30 mins	32 mins	35 mins	40 mins

PLEASE NOTE: Baking times for sponges baked in pudding basins and loaf tins may take longer.

BAKING TEST When the sponge has reached the recommended baking time, open the oven door slowly and, if the sponge is pale in colour, continue baking until light brown. When light brown, run your fingers across the top gently and the sponge should spring back when touched. If not then continue baking and test every few minutes.

STORAGE When cold the sponge can be deep-frozen for up to six months. Use within three days of baking or defrosting.

PORTIONS A 20.5cm (8in) round sponge should provide approximately sixteen portions when decorated.

For chocolate flavoured sponges:

For every 115g (4oz) of flour used in the recipe add the following ingredients: 2tbsp of cocoa powder dissolved in 2tbsp of hot water, leave to cool then add to the other ingredients in step 3.

For coffee flavoured sponges:

For every 115g (4oz) of flour used in the recipe add 2tsp of instant coffee dissolved in 1tbsp of boiling water, leave to cool then add to the other ingredients in step 3.

For orange or lemon flavoured sponges:

For every 115g (4oz) of flour used in the recipe add the grated rind of one orange or lemon to the other ingredients in step 3.

INGREDIENTS *for Two 20.5cm round sponges (8in) or two 18cm square sponges (7in).*

170g self-raising flour (6oz)
1½ tsp baking powder
170g soft (tub) margarine (6oz)
170g caster sugar (6oz)
3 eggs, size 3

BAKING

Bake in a pre-heated oven at 170°C (325°F) or Gas Mark 3 for approximately 30 minutes.

EQUIPMENT

Two 20.5cm round sponge tins (8in)
OR two 18cm square sponge tins (7in)
Soft (tub) margarine for greasing
Brush
Greaseproof paper
Mixing bowl
Sieve
Beater
Spatula

1 Grease the tins with soft (tub) margarine, line the bases with greaseproof paper then grease the paper.

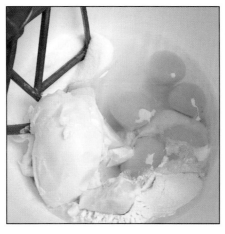

2 Sift the flour and baking powder together twice to ensure a thorough mix. Then place into a mixing bowl with all the other ingredients.

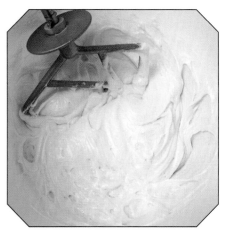

3 Beat mixture for 3-4 minutes until light in colour.

4 Spread the mixture evenly between the two tins. Bake in pre-heated oven (see baking test).

5 When the sponges are baked, leave to cool in the tins for 5 minutes, then carefully turn out onto a wire tray until cold.

6 When cold, sandwich the sponges together with jam and cream then place into a refrigerator for 1 hour before decorating.

MADEIRA SPONGE CAKE

For hexagonal, octagonal or petal shaped madeira cakes use recipe for the equivalent round cake. Example, for 20.5cm (8in) heart shape use ingredients for 20.5cm (8in) round sponge cake.

Square tin OR	12.5cm (5in)	15cm (6in)	18cm (7in)	20.5cm (8in)	23cm (9in)	25.5cm (10in)	28cm (11in)
Round tin	15cm (6in)	18cm (7in)	20.5cm (8in)	23cm (9in)	25.5cm (10in)	28cm (11in)	30.5cm (12in)
Butter	60g (2oz)	115g (4oz)	170g (6oz)	225g (8oz)	285g (10oz)	340g (12oz)	400g (14oz)
Caster sugar	60g (2oz)	115g (4oz)	170g (6oz)	225g (8oz)	285g (10oz)	340g (12oz)	400g (14oz)
Eggs, size 2	1	2	3	4	5	6	7
Plain flour	30g (1oz)	60g (2oz)	85g (3oz)	115g (4oz)	145g (5oz)	170g (6oz)	200g (7oz)
Self-raising flour	60g (2oz)	115g (4oz)	170g (6oz)	225g (8oz)	285g (10oz)	340g (12oz)	400g (14oz)
Lemons	¼	½	1	1	1½	1½	2
Baking temperature				170°C (325°F) or Gas Mark 3			
Approximate baking time	¾hr	1hr	1¼hrs	1¼hrs	1¼hrs	1½hrs	1½hrs

CURDLING

Curdling can occur if eggs are added too quickly to the cake mixture or if there is insufficient beating between the additions. If curdling does occur, immediately beat in a small amount of flour until the batter is smooth and then continue adding egg, a little at a time. Should curdling re-occur simply add a little more flour.

BAKING TEST Bring the cake forward in the oven at the end of the recommended baking time so that it can be tested. Insert a stainless steel skewer into the centre of the cake and slowly withdraw it. If the cake is sufficiently baked, the skewer will come out of the cake as cleanly as it went in. Continue baking at the same temperature if the cake mixture clings to the skewer. Test every ten minutes until the skewer is clean when withdrawn from the cake.

FREEZING Madeira sponge cake can be frozen for up to six months. Make sure that it is completely thawed before use.

STORAGE Use within three days of baking or defrosting.

PORTIONS A 20.5cm (8in) round madeira sponge cake should serve approximately sixteen portions when decorated.

INGREDIENTS

170g butter (6oz)
170g caster sugar (6oz)
3 eggs, size 2
85g plain flour (3oz)
170g self-raising flour (6oz)
1 lemon

EQUIPMENT

18cm square cake tin (7in)
OR 20.5cm round cake tin (8in)
Butter for greasing
Greaseproof paper
Mixing bowl
Mixing spoon
Spatula

BAKING

Bake in a pre-heated oven at 170°C
(325°F) or Gas Mark 3 for 1¼hrs.

1 Grease the tin lightly with butter, fully line with greaseproof paper, then grease the paper.

2 Sift the flours together. Cream the butter and sugar together until light and fluffy.

3 Stir the egg(s) together before beating a little at a time into the creamed mixture (see curdling).

4 Lightly fold the sifted flours into the mixture together with the lemon rind and juice.

5 Place mixture into the tin, and using a spatula, level the top. Bake for recommended time.

6 See baking test instructions. When baked, leave in the tin to cool for 10 minutes before turning out onto a wire rack to cool completely.

ALL-IN-ONE FRUIT CAKE

This fruit cake makes the ideal base for any sugarpaste or royal icing celebration cake and has excellent keeping properties. When making a fruit cake, it requires at least three weeks to mature.

For hexagonal, octagonal or petal shaped cakes use recipe for the equivalent round cake. Example, for 20.5cm (8in) heart shape use ingredients for 20.5cm (8in) round cake.

Square tin OR	12.5cm (5in)	15cm (6in)	18cm (7in)	20.5cm (8in)	23cm (9in)	25.5cm (10in)	28cm (11in)
Round tin	15cm (6in)	18cm (7in)	20.5cm (8in)	23cm (9in)	25.5cm (10in)	28cm (11in)	30.5cm (12in)
Sultanas	85g (3oz)	115g (4oz)	170g (6oz)	225g (8oz)	285g (10oz)	340g (12oz)	425g (15oz)
Currants	85g (3oz)	115g (4oz)	170g (6oz)	225g (8oz)	285g (10oz)	340g (12oz)	425g (15oz)
Raisins	85g (3oz)	115g (4oz)	170g (6oz)	225g (8oz)	285g (10oz)	340g (12oz)	425g (15oz)
Candied peel	30g (1oz)	60g (2oz)	60g (2oz)	85g (3oz)	85g (3oz)	115g (4oz)	170g (6oz)
Glacé cherries	30g (1oz)	60g (2oz)	60g (2oz)	85g (3oz)	85g (3oz)	115g (4oz)	170g (6oz)
Lemon rind (lemons)	¼	½	½	1	1½	2	2
Rum/Brandy	½tbsp	½tbsp	1tbsp	1tbsp	1½tbsp	2tbsp	2tbsp
Black treacle	½tbsp	½tbsp	1tbsp	1tbsp	1½tbsp	2tbsp	2tbsp
Soft (tub) margarine	85g (3oz)	115g (4oz)	170g (6oz)	225g (8oz)	285g (10oz)	340g (12oz)	425g (15oz)
Soft light brown sugar	85g (3oz)	115g (4oz)	170g (6oz)	225g (8oz)	285g (10oz)	340g (12oz)	425g (15oz)
Eggs, size 3	1½	2	3	4	5	6	7½
Ground almonds	15g (½oz)	30g (1oz)	45g (1½oz)	60g (2oz)	70g (2½oz)	85g (3oz)	115g (4oz)
Self-raising flour	115g (4oz)	145g (5oz)	200g (7oz)	255g (9oz)	315g (11oz)	400g (14oz)	515g (18oz)
Ground mace	pinch	pinch	pinch	pinch	pinch	pinch	pinch
Mixed spice	¼tsp	½tsp	½tsp	¾tsp	1tsp	1¼tsp	1½tsp
Ground nutmeg	pinch	pinch	¼tsp	¼tsp	½tsp	½tsp	¾tsp
Baking temperature	----150°C (300°F) or Gas Mark 2---			-----------140°C (275°F) or Gas Mark 1-----------			
Approximate baking time	1¾hrs	2hrs	2½hrs	3hrs	3½hrs	4½hrs	6hrs

BAKING TEST Bring the cake forward from the oven at the end of the recommended baking time so that it can be tested. Insert a stainless steel skewer into the centre of the cake and slowly withdraw it. If the cake is sufficiently baked, the skewer will come out as clean as it went in.

Continue baking at the same temperature if the cake mixture clings to the skewer. Test in the same way every ten minutes until the skewer is clean when withdrawn from the cake.

INGREDIENTS

225g sultanas (8oz)　　225g soft (tub) margarine (8oz)
225g currants (8oz)　　225g soft light brown sugar (8oz)
225g raisins (8oz)　　4 eggs, size 3
85g candied peel (3oz)　　60g ground almonds (2oz)
85g glacé cherries (3oz)　　255g self-raising flour (9oz)
1 lemon　　Pinch of ground mace
1tbsp rum/brandy　　¾tsp mixed spice
1tbsp black treacle　　¼tsp ground nutmeg

EQUIPMENT

20.5cm square cake tin (8in)
OR 23cm round cake tin (9in)
Soft (tub) margarine for greasing
Greaseproof paper
Mixing bowl
Beater
Sieve
Mixing spoon
Skewer

PREPARATION of INGREDIENTS

Weigh all the ingredients separately. Chop cherries in half and carefully clean and remove stalks from all the fruit. Grate the lemon and then mix all the fruit together with rum/brandy. Sift the flour, nutmeg, spice and mace together three times. For better results leave overnight in a warm place 18°C (65°F).

PREPARATION of the CAKE TIN

Cut out a length of greasproof paper deeper than the cake tin (enough to cover inside) and then cut along bottom edges at 2.5cm (1in) intervals. Cut a circle or square as required for the base of the tin.
Brush the inside of the tin with soft margarine. Then cover the side with greaseproof paper and place the circle or square into the bottom of the tin. Finally brush the greaseproof paper with margarine.

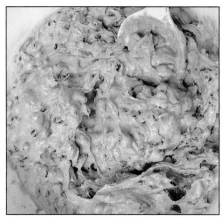

1 Prepare the tin, fruit and other ingredients as described above. Pre-heat the oven. Place all ingredients, except the fruit, into a mixing bowl. Beat together for 2-3 minutes.

2 Using a spoon, blend in the fruit until well mixed. Place mixture into the tin, level the top and bake.

3 After recommended baking time follow baking test instructions. When baked, leave in the tin until cold. See instructions for storage.

BAKING

Bake in a pre-heated oven at 140°C (275°F) or Gas mark 1 for approximately 2½ to 3hrs.

STORAGE
Remove the cake carefully from the tin when it is cold and then take off the greaseproof paper. Wrap the cake in waxed paper and leave in a cupboard for at least three weeks.

PORTIONS
To estimate the number of portions that can be cut from a finished cake, add up the total weight of all the cake ingredients, almond paste, sugarpaste and/or royal icing. As the average slice of a finished cake weighs approximately 60g (2oz), simply divide the total weight accordingly to calculate the number of portions.

ALL-IN-ONE SWISS ROLL

Swiss Rolls are easy to make and form a useful and versatile base for a cake. They can be filled with a variety of fillings and then coated in buttercream or cream, flavoured and coloured if required. Swiss Rolls can also be covered in sugarpaste over a layer of buttercream.

BAKING

Bake in a pre-heated oven at 200°C (400°F) or Gas mark 6 for approximately 10-12 minutes.

STORAGE The filled sponge may be wrapped in waxed paper and deep-frozen for up to 6 months. Use within 3 days of baking or after defrosting.

BAKING TEST When the sponge has been baking for the recommended time, open the oven door slowly and, if the sponge is pale in colour, continue baking. When the sponge is golden brown, draw fingers across the top (pressing lightly) and, if this action leaves an indentation, continue baking. Repeat test every 1-2 minutes until the top springs back when touched.

INGREDIENTS

60g soft (tub) margarine (2oz)
115g caster sugar (4oz)
115g egg (4oz)
115g self-raising flour (4oz)

FILLING

Softened jam or preserve of choice.

EQUIPMENT and PREPARATION

18 x 28cm swiss roll tin (7 x 11in)
Pastry brush
Margarine
Greaseproof paper
Mixing bowl
Palette knife
Tea towel
Caster sugar
Wire cooling tray

1 Lightly grease the swiss roll tin with the margarine and fully line with greaseproof paper. Then grease the greaseproof paper with margarine.

2 Place all the ingredients into a mixing bowl. Beat together until light, white and creamy. Using a spatula spread the mixture evenly in the tin.

3 Bake in a pre-heated oven (see baking and baking test). Whilst the sponge is baking, place greaseproof paper onto a tea towel and sprinkle with caster sugar.

4 When baked, immediately turn the sponge out onto the sugared paper. Carefully remove the lining paper.

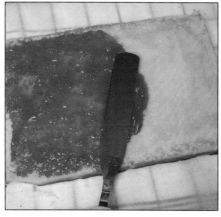

5 After a few minutes spread filling of choice with a palette knife. It is important to spread the filling before the sponge becomes too cold.

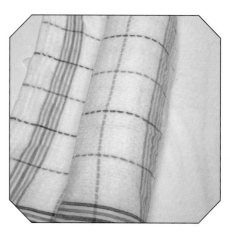

6 Tightly roll up the sponge, using the towel to keep the pressure even. When cool, remove the towel and place the swiss roll onto a wire tray to cool completely (see notes).

ALMOND PASTE

Almond paste is a mixture of uncooked ground almonds, sugar and glucose or eggs. Whereas marzipan is made from cooked ground almonds and sugar. Almond paste can be stored in waxed paper or in a sealed container in a cool, dry place. Do not overmix when making the almond paste. Do not allow the almond paste to come into contact with flour as fermentation may occur.

The almond paste stage in cake decorating is vital in ensuring that smooth layers of icing can be applied later.

Carefully prepare cakes for covering by levelling the top of a domed shape cake or removing the outer edges of a sunken cake. Fill in any imperfections with almond paste and remove any burnt fruit from the surface.

Use icing sugar or caster sugar at all times when rolling out almond paste.

Use boiling apricot purée when fixing almond paste to the cake as this will help prevent mould or fermentation.

When covering a cake, ensure that the layer of almond paste is thick enough to prevent dis-colouring. When covered with almond paste, the cake should have a level top and vertical sides.

After the cake has been covered with almond paste, it should be left to stand in a warm room at about 18°C (65°F) for three to four days. Do not store covered cakes in sealed containers.

To colour almond paste: Blend in food or paste colours. Do not overmix.

USE INGREDIENTS **A** FOR RECIPE WITH EGGS OR
INGREDIENTS **B** FOR RECIPE WITHOUT EGGS

INGREDIENTS A

115g caster sugar (4oz)
115g icing sugar (4oz)
225g ground almonds (8oz)
1tsp fresh lemon juice
Few drops of almond essence
1 egg, size 3 or
2 egg yolks, size 3, beaten

INGREDIENTS B

170g icing sugar (6oz)
170g caster sugar (6oz)
340g ground almonds (12oz)
225g glucose syrup, warmed (8oz)

1 **For either recipe:** mix the dry ingredients together and stir to form an even, crumbly texture.

2 Make a well in the centre, then add the remaining ingredients and mix to a firm but pliable paste.

3 Turn out onto a working surface, dusted lightly with caster or icing sugar, and knead until smooth. Store in a sealed container until required.

BUTTER ICING

INGREDIENTS

115g butter, at room temperature
(4oz)
170-225g icing sugar, sifted (6-8oz)
Few drops vanilla extract
1-2tbsp milk

This recipe can be flavoured and
coloured as desired.

1 For the butter icing: beat the
butter until light and fluffy.

2 Beat in the icing sugar, a little at a
time, adding the vanilla extract and
sufficient milk to give a fairly firm
but spreading consistency.

MODELLING PASTE

INGREDIENTS

255g icing sugar (9oz)
1 level tbsp gum tragacanth
1 level tsp liquid glucose
8tsp cold water

STORAGE

Store in a refrigerator using a food-
approved polythene bag in an airtight
container. Always bring to room
temperature before use.

1 Thoroughly sift together the icing
sugar and gum tragacanth into a
mixing bowl

2 Blend the glucose and water
together then pour into the dry
ingredients and mix well.

3 Knead the mixture by hand until a
smooth and pliable paste is formed.
To store, see instructions above.

SUGARPASTE

INGREDIENTS

2tbsp cold water
1½ level tsp powdered gelatine
1½ tbsp liquid glucose
2tsp glycerin
450g icing sugar, sifted (1lb)

MODELLING PASTE

Add 2tsp of gum tragacanth to the basic sugarpaste recipe and work well in.
Leave for 24 hours before use.
Store as sugarpaste.

COLOURING SUGARPASTE

Add food colour a little at a time and mix well in until the required colour is achieved. Always make sufficient coloured sugarpaste as it is difficult to match colour later.

MOTTLED SUGARPASTE

Partially mix food colouring into sugarpaste. Then roll out.

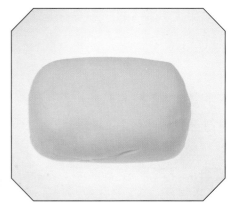

1 Pour the water into a saucepan and sprinkle on the powdered gelatine. Dissolve over low heat. Stir in the glucose and glycerin then remove from the heat.

2 Gradually add and stir in the icing sugar with a spoon to avoid making a lumpy mixture. When unable to stir anymore icing sugar into mixture, turn out onto table.

3 Mix in the remaining icing sugar using fingers then knead until a pliable smooth paste is formed. Store in a sealed container until required.

COVERING CAKES

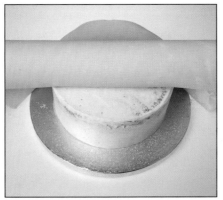

1 Coat the cake-side and top with a thin layer of butter icing. Chill for 1 hour in the refrigerator.

2 When chilled, roll out the sugarpaste and place over the cake, using a rolling pin.

3 Smooth the paste over the top, then down the side, using palm of hand. Trim around the cake-base or board edge. Leave until dry before decorating.

ROYAL ICING

1 For albumen solution: pour the water into a bowl, then stir and sprinkle in the albumen powder. Whisk slowly to half-blend in. The solution will go lumpy. Leave for 1 hour, stirring occasionally.

2 Pour the solution through a fine sieve or muslin. It is now ready for use. Store in a sealed container and keep in a cool place until required.

ALBUMEN SOLUTION

INGREDIENTS

15g pure albumen powder (½oz)
85g cold water (3oz)

ROYAL ICING

INGREDIENTS

100g fresh egg whites or albumen solution (3½oz)
450g icing sugar, sifted (1lb)

If using fresh egg whites, separate 24 hours before use.

FOR SOFT CUTTING ROYAL ICING

For every 450g (1lb) ready-made royal icing beat in the following amounts of glycerin:

1tsp for bottom tier of three tiered cake.
2tsp for middle tiers.
3tsp for top tiers, single tiers and general piping.

DO NOT ADD GLYCERIN WHEN MAKING RUNOUTS, FIGURE PIPING, PIPED FLOWERS AND LEAVES OR FINE LINE WORK.

1 For making royal icing: pour the egg whites or albumen solution into a bowl. Slowly mix in half the icing sugar until dissolved.

2 Then slowly mix in the remaining sugar. Run a spatula around the inside of the bowl to ensure all the ingredients are blended together.

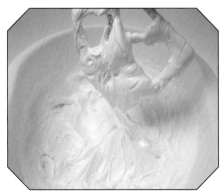

3 Thoroughly beat mixture until light and fluffy. Peaks should be formed when the spoon or beater is lifted. Clean down inside then cover with a damp cloth until required.

EQUIPMENT

You will find that many of the items needed for cake decorating are already in your kitchen or can be improvised if necessary. However, if you are buying equipment, do buy the best quality available as, with care, this should last a lifetime.

Where possible, keep decorating utensils for this job only as icing and sugarpaste can easily become tainted or discoloured by food particles, odours, grease or rust. Food approved plastic, stainless steel and glass bowls are ideal and cake tins should be strong and rigid.

Before commencing work, gather together all the equipment you will need. All equipment should be scrupulously clean and free from grease. An electric mixer saves a great deal of time and energy, but is not essential for success.

You will need a heavy, smooth rolling pin for sugarpaste and nylon spacers make achieving an even thickness much easier. Spacers can also be used for marking the paste, as can clean steel or plastic rulers, but any straight plastic edge of appropriate thickness will do.

A fine sponge is useful for creating texture. The type used in the bathroom is ideal, as long as it is fresh and clean. Sponges used for other purposes should be avoided.

Cake boards are important. Always use the thicker type of the stipulated size to hold the cake. Card cards, which are much thinner, are not suitable for supporting weight. Cake boards can be covered in decorative paper, but this should be food-approved or should be covered in non-stick paper or a small cake card. A cake should never be placed directly onto a non-food-approved covering.

A turntable makes decorating much easier but this is not essential as it can be improvised by an upturned plate or cake tin. A good turntable is large and solid enough to support a heavy cake, with a minimum diameter of 23cm (9in). It should have a non-slip base and be easy to turn.

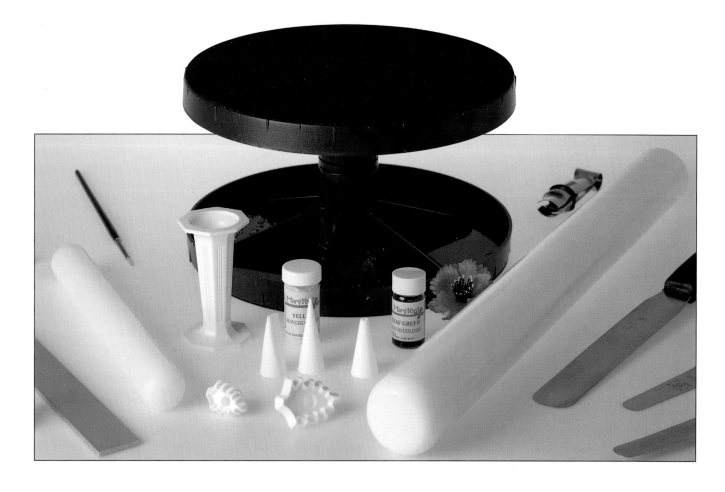

HINTS AND TIPS

BAKING

Weigh all ingredients carefully, particularly when using the all-in-one recipe.

Never use eggs straight out of the refrigerator. Allow to reach room temperature.

All ingredients should preferably be at room temperature.

Always use the correct size tin for the amount of batter.

Cakes should be baked on the centre shelf of the oven unless specified.

CURDLING

Curdling can occur if eggs are added too quickly to the cake mixture or if there is insufficient beating between the additions. If curdling does occur, immediately beat in a small amount of flour until the batter is smooth and then continue adding egg, a little at a time.

BUTTER ICING

To obtain best results, always use fresh butter at a temperature of 18-21°C (65-70°F).

COLOURING and PAINTING

Add a little colour at a time when colouring sugarpaste or royal icing.

Most paste colours dry darker.

If mixing a large quantity, leave overnight to settle before use.

Always colour sufficient icing or sugarpaste to complete the decoration as it is virtually impossible to match the colour. Taste coloured sugarpaste or royal icing before use as too much colour will make it bitter.

Let sugarpaste dry thoroughly before painting.

When painting, use a very small amount of colour on the tip of a fine paintbrush.

To colour granulated sugar: place in a bowl, add a drop of colouring. Stir well with a spoon. Turn onto greaseproof paper to dry. Store in a jar.

DECORATIVE BOARD COVERING

Decorative board covering can be wallpaper samples, or patterned paper, wrapping paper is ideal, glued to the cake board. Use a cake card between the covering and the cake.

SUGARPASTE

Sugarpaste can be purchased ready-made if required.

Sugarpaste should be made 24 hours before use.

If the paste is too dry, add a little white fat or egg white.

If the paste is too sticky, add a little cornflour or icing sugar.

In cold weather, warm the paste slightly in the oven.

If a crust has formed, remove before use.

Protect coloured sugarpaste from strong light.

Sugarpaste can be flavoured with a drop or two of flavouring to counteract sweetness.

Roll out sugarpaste on an icing sugar dusted surface.

The drying time for sugarpaste varies with the weather and conditions in the kitchen. 24 hours is an approximate time. Sugarpaste should be crimped before it dries.

When crimping, hold the crimper at right angles to the cake and push gently into the paste before squeezing the crimper. Release the pressure and remove carefully.

MODELLING PASTE

Always work with clean, dry hands and surfaces in a cool, dry atmosphere. Icing sugar or a mixture of icing sugar and cornflour can be used to prevent sticking. Once dry, detail can be piped in or painted using edible food colours and a fine paint brush. Never paint with liquid or paste colour direct from the bottle. Place a little of the colour on greaseproof paper and wipe any excess off the brush before use. Allow colours to dry before overpainting with another colour.

FIXING

Butter icing or jam should be used to join sponge cakes.

Use cooled boiled water or clear liquor when fixing sugarpaste to sugarpaste.

Use royal icing or cooled boiled water when fixing sugarpaste figures to sugarpaste.

Fix ribbons with small dots or fine lines of royal icing.

Fix rice paper with a minute amount of cooled, boiled water, egg white or piping gel.

Fix modelling paste with cool boiled water, egg white, gum arabic solution or royal icing.

STIPPLING

Use a palette knife to stipple large areas or a sponge for small, fine areas.

FRILL

Frill sugarpaste by rolling the pointed end of a cocktail stick or paintbrush along the edge a little at a time.

PORTIONS

A 20.5cm (8in) round sponge will provide approximately 16 portions.

FREEZING

Batch baked swiss rolls and sponges can be frozen for up to six months. Swiss rolls can be rolled up before freezing and stored unfilled.

INGREDIENTS

Large swiss roll
1.25k sugarpaste (2½lb)
170g royal icing (6oz)
Pink dusting powder
Pink, caramel and black
 food colours
Piping tube No.1

EQUIPMENT and DECORATIONS

35.5cm oval cake board (14in)
Paint brush
Serrated scraper
Modelling tools
Board edge ribbon

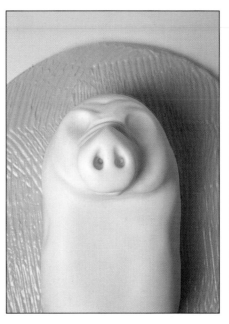

1 Cover the board with royal icing, then create the effect shown with a serrated scraper. Trim the sponge and cover with sugarpaste forming the head at the same time.

2 Mould and fix the eyes, then colour the face with dusting powder.

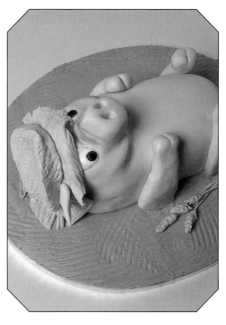

3 Mould four sugarpaste limbs as shown. Make a curly tail.

4 Fix pieces to the body as shown.

5 Make and fix a sugarpaste hat and straws. Pipe inscription of choice (No.1).

FISHING BOAT

INGREDIENTS

30.5cm square cake (12in)
Piece of cake or sponge for boat
2.5k almond paste (5lb)
2k sugarpaste (4lb)
225g royal icing (8oz)
Assorted food colours

EQUIPMENT and DECORATIONS

40.5cm square cake board (16in)
Fine paint brush
Tweezers
Spaghetti strand
Board edge ribbon
Piping tube No.1

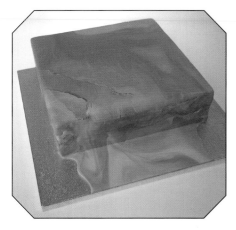

1 Fix the cake to the back edge of the board then cover the cake with mottled sugarpaste, including the front section of the board.

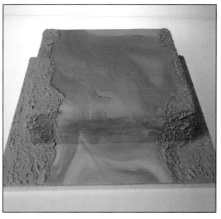

2 Stipple each side of the cake and remaining board surface with royal icing to create the banks.

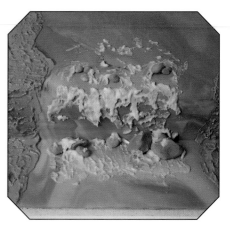

3 Mould sugarpaste into rocks, fix to the front edge of the cake, then stipple royal icing to form the waterfall.

4 Shape the extra cake into the boat, then cover with sugarpaste marked as shown.

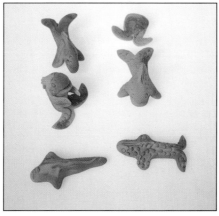

5 Mould mottled coloured sugarpaste into fish in various shapes.

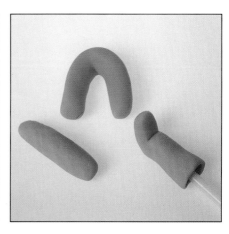

6 Mould trousers and boots for the fisherman with sugarpaste.

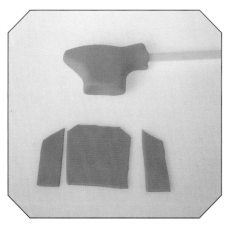

7 Mould the waistcoat and shirt as shown.

8 Fix the pieces together in a sitting position, using sugarpaste or polystyrene for support.

9 Mould and fix head, hat and hands.

27

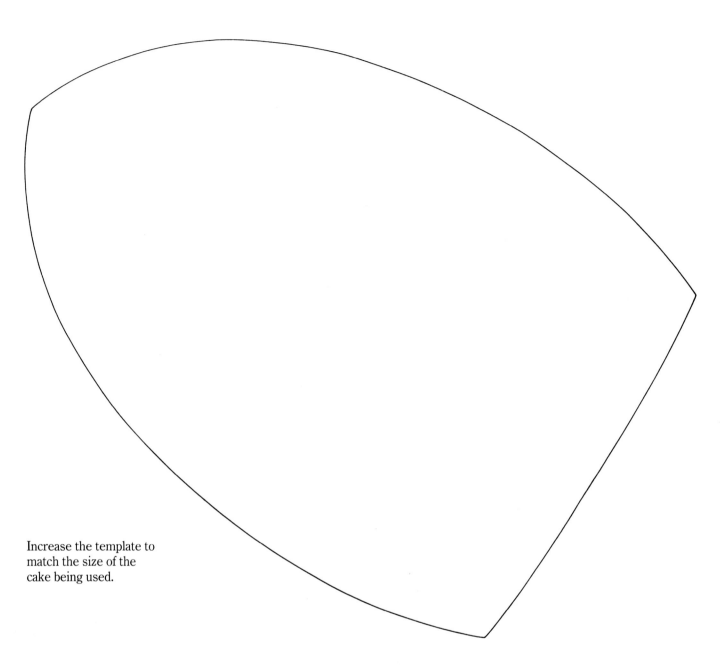

Increase the template to
match the size of the
cake being used.

10 Make a sugarpaste seat then fix
to the boat with the fisherman.
Make and fix basket and flask.

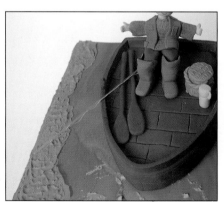

11 Make and fix sugarpaste oars.
Fix a spaghetti strand for the
fishing rod, then pipe the line
around the rod as shown (No.1).

12 Fix the fish around the boat as
required.

RUGGER

INGREDIENTS

20.5cm round sponge (8in)
900g sugarpaste (2lb)
340g royal icing (12oz)
Assorted food colours

EQUIPMENT and DECORATIONS

45.5 x 35.5cm oblong cake board
 (18 x 14in)
Coarse cloth
Modelling tool
Piping tube No.1
Board edge ribbon

1 Trim the sponge to the rugby ball shape, cover with sugarpaste and mark with a coarse cloth. Using a modelling tool, create the stitching.

2 Stipple the board with mottled royal icing. Fix the sponge, then roll out and fix sugarpaste posts.

3 Mould and fix a sugarpaste boot. Make and fix a scarf. Decorate with piped lines and inscirption of choice (No.1).

INGREDIENTS

Large swiss roll
Small swiss roll, 4 required
Sponge baked in a 600ml
 pudding basin (1pt)
115g royal icing (4oz)
Assorted food colours

EQUIPMENT and DECORATIONS

28cm square cake board (11in)
Plastic dowel
Piping tube No.1
Paint brush
Candles and holders
Board edge ribbon

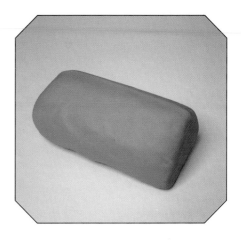

1 Cover the large swiss roll with sugarpaste for the body.

2 Cover a small swiss roll with sugarpaste and leave excess as shown for a leg.

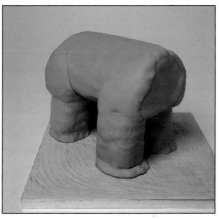

3 Support the body, then fix the leg under and against the body, as shown.

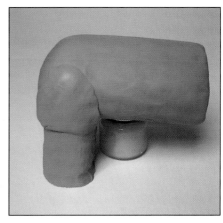

4 Repeat for each leg. Remove the support when firm. Coat the board with royal icing and fix the body.

5 Trim the sponge to head shape. Cover with sugarpaste forming the trunk as shown. Fix to the body with plastic dowel. Mark trunk with back of knife.

6 Make and fix sugarpaste ears, eyes, tusks and toes.

7 Decorate the elephant with sugarpaste blankets and head-dress. Fix candles, then pipe inscription with royal icing (No.1).

31

20.5cm round sponge (8in)
 2 required
1.5k sugarpaste (3lb)
115g royal icing (4oz)
Confectioner's varnish
Assorted food colours

35.5cm round cake board (14in)
25.5cm round cake board (10in)
Decorative board covering
Crimper
Fine paint brush
Coarse sieve
Piping tube No.2
Board edge ribbon

1 Cover the large board with decorative paper. Layer the sponges together. Cover the sponge and small cake board with sugarpaste. Crimp around the cake-top edge and board. Cut out and fix sugarpaste sauce.

2 Cut sugarpaste chips and colour to give cooked effect. Cut a length of sugarpaste and mould into bean shapes.

3 Fix the chips to the cake-top. Fix the beans to the sauce then brush with confectioner's varnish. Extra chips and beans will be required for the sandwich.

4 Make two fried eggs with sugarpaste and fix to the cake-top then brush the yolks with varnish.

5 Roll out a piece of sugarpaste and press with a coarse sieve, then cut out and fix the crust to form the slice of bread. 2 slices required.

6 Spread royal icing onto the slices and fix one to the cake-side. Place chips and beans into the remaining slice, fold in half and fix to the cake-side. Pipe inscription of choice with royal icing (No.2).

TOY SHOP

INGREDIENTS

20.5cm round sponge (8in)
20.5cm square sponge (8in)
 2 required
1.5k sugarpaste (3lb)
Gelatine sheets
225g modelling paste (8oz)
Granulated sugar
Assorted food colours

EQUIPMENT and DECORATIONS

30.5cm square cake board (12in)
Cake card
Paint brush
Cocktail stick
Crimped cutter
Piping tube No.43
Board edge ribbon

34

1 Layer the square sponges together and place upright. Cut the round sponge in half, layer and fix to the front. Cover all with sugarpaste.

2 Fix the cake to the board. Stipple the remaining board surface with royal icing. Make and fix mottled sugarpaste stones.

3 Make a selection of sugarpaste toys and figures.

4 Fix to the window and decorate as required. Paint the brick work.

5 Cut and fix gelatine sheets to form the windows, using sugarpaste for the frames.

6 Cut cake card to size required for roof and cover with royal icing. Sprinkle with granulated sugar, then fix to the cake-top. Pipe the shells (No.43).

7 Make the figure of a girl as shown, using modelling paste. Support until dry.

8 Make the figure of a lady as shown, using modelling paste. Support until dry.

9 Make the figure of a man as shown, using modelling paste. Support until dry. Fix the figures to the board. Decorate the roof as required.

THE MUMMY

INGREDIENTS

23cm square sponge (9in) 2 required
1.5k sugarpaste (3lb)
115g royal icing (4oz)
Red, blue, black and peach food colours

EQUIPMENT and DECORATIONS

40.5cm oval cake board (16in)
Decorative board covering
Piping tube No.1

36

1 Using the template as a guide, cut and layer the sponges to the basic mummy shape. Coat with butter icing and chill for 1 hour.

2 Make and fix sugarpaste eyes, nose and mouth.

3 Roll out sugarpaste and cut into strips. Cover the sponge in a criss-cross manner as shown. Roll up a length of sugarpaste and form into bandage. Pipe on the message with royal icing (No.1).

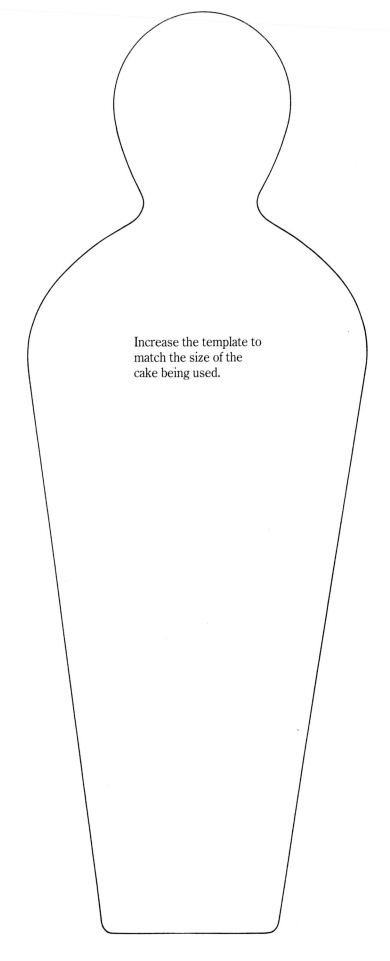

Increase the template to match the size of the cake being used.

THE MAD HATTER

20.5cm oval sponge (8in) 2 required
Sponge baked in a 600ml pudding
 basin (1pt)
225g royal icing (8oz)
1.5k sugarpaste (3lb)
Pink dusting powder
Assorted food colours
Spaghetti strands

EQUIPMENT and DECORATIONS

30.5cm oval cake board (12in)
Cocktail stick
Paint brush
Piping tube No.1
Dowel
Floral wire
Board edge ribbon

1 Stipple the board with royal icing.
Make and fix the two sugarpaste
feet shown.

2 Layer the sponges together, then
trim to body shape. Cover with
sugarpaste, then fix to the board.

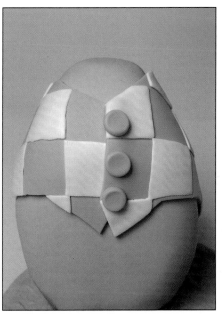

3 Cut out and fix a sugarpaste
waistcoat and buttons.

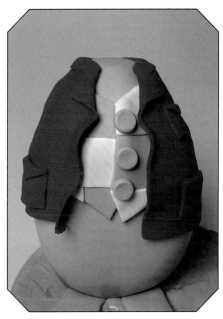

4 Cut out and fix a sugarpaste jacket
and pockets. Turn the paste over at
the top to form the collar.

39

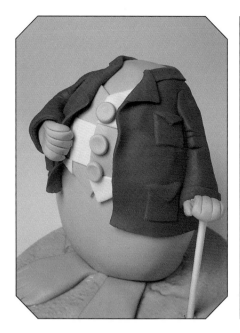

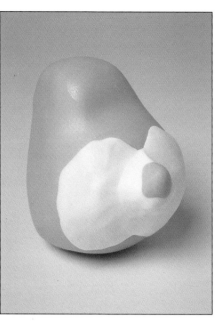

5 Mould and fix arms and hands. Place a length of dowel under the hand as shown.

6 Trim the pudding shape sponge for the head, then cover with sugarpaste. Cut out and fix sugarpaste cheeks and nose.

7 Mould and fix sugarpaste ridge and eyes. Scratch the paste with a cocktail stick to create fur effect. Brush with dusting powder, then insert spaghetti strands.

8 Mould and fix sugarpaste floppy ears.

9 Make and fix a sugarpaste hat in manner shown. Decorate with ribbon and price tag.

10 Make and fix a sugarpaste watch. Pipe the chain with royal icing (No.1). Cover the dowel with sugarpaste for the walking stick. Twist wire for the glasses.

BIRTHDAY GALLEON

INGREDIENTS

25.5cm square sponge (10in)
 2 required
1.5 sugarpaste (3lb)
115g royal icing (4oz)
Assorted dusting powders
Edible food colour pens
Assorted food colours

EQUIPMENT and DECORATIONS

56 x 30.5cm oblong cake board
 (22 x 12in)
Decorative board covering
Rice paper
Piping tube No.1
Ribbon
Board edge ribbon

1 Trim the sponges and cover with sugarpaste, then fix to the covered board. Mark the sides with a knife to resemble pages. Brush the sides with dusting powder.

2 Using the templates as a guide, draw the gifts and sea onto rice paper. Colour as required, then cut out and fix to the cake-top.

3 Using the templates as a guide, draw the galleon onto rice paper. Colour as required, then cut out and fix to the cake-top.

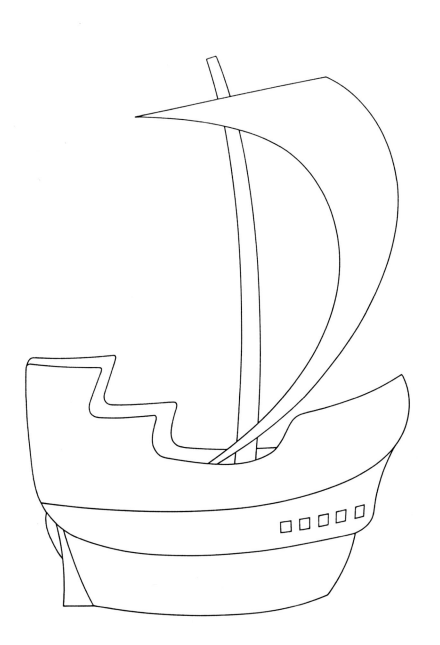

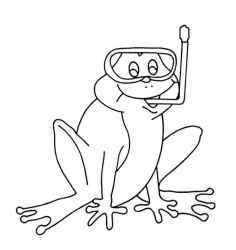

4 Using the templates as a guide, draw the seals and animals onto rice paper. Colour as required, then cut out and fix to the cake-top.

5 Using the template as a guide, draw the whale onto rice paper. Colour as required, then cut out and fix to the cake-top.

6 Using the templates as a guide, draw the remaining shapes onto rice paper. Colour as required, then cut out and fix to the cake-top. Pipe inscription of choice (No.1). Fix ribbon.

INGREDIENTS

25.5cm oval sponge (10in)
900g sugarpaste (2lb)
225g modelling paste (8oz)
115g royal icing (4oz)
Assorted food colours

EQUIPMENT and DECORATIONS

35.5cm oval cake board (14in)
Piping tube No.1
Rule
Board edge ribbon

1 Place the sponge to the top of the board then cover all with mottled sugarpaste. Mark with a rule to resemble floor planks.

2 Make a selection of sports equipment, mats and towels.

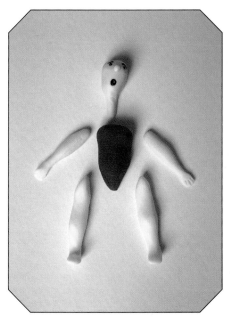

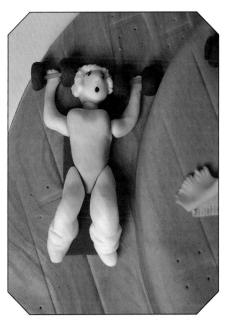

3 Mould the various parts of a person, using modelling paste.

4 Fix the pieces together as shown, then pipe the hair with royal icing.

5 Repeat steps 3 and 4 varying the shapes and colours for other sporting figures. Fix to the cake and board. Pipe inscription of choice (No.1).

FATHER'S DAY

INGREDIENTS

25.5cm oval shaped cake (10in)
1.25k almond paste (2½lb)
1.5k sugarpaste (3lb)
115g royal icing (4oz)
Sponge fingers
Yellow and pink dusting powder
Snowflake dusting powder
Assorted food colours

EQUIPMENT and DECORATIONS

35.5cm oval shaped cake
 board (14in)
Ribbed roller or rule
Crimper
Paint brush
Piping tubes No.1 and 4
Board edge ribbon

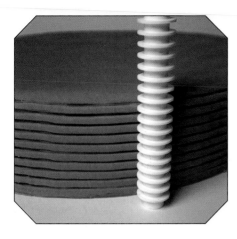

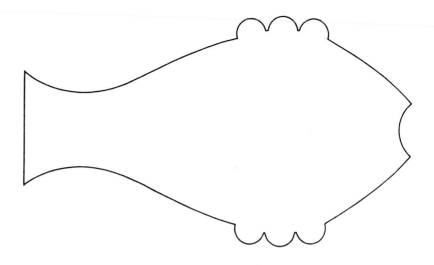

1 Cover cake with sugarpaste. Immediately roll the side with a roller or mark with a rule.

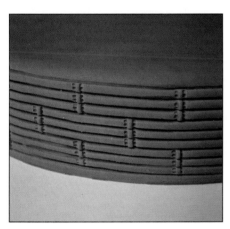

2 Crimp across the lines to achieve a basket effect.

3 Fix the cake to the board then stipple with royal icing. Twist two lengths of sugarpaste together then fix around the cake-base.

4 Twist two more lengths of sugarpaste together and fix around the cake-top edge as shown. Lightly brush with brown colour.

5 Cover a sponge finger with sugarpaste to form a fish shape. Mark the mouth and gill with a knife. Using a No.4 piping tube, mark the eye and fish scales.

6 Make and fix fins then colour with snowflake dusting powder. Make as many fish as required.

7 Place the fish onto the cake-top and board. Cut out a fish sugarpaste plaque. Pipe inscription of choice with royal icing (No.1).

ONE ARMED BANDIT

INGREDIENTS

25.5cm square sponge (10in)
Miniature swiss roll
600g sugarpaste (2lb)
115g royal icing (4oz)
Assorted food colours

EQUIPMENT and DECORATIONS

25.5cm round cake board (10in)
Rule
Assorted cutters
Piping tubes No.1 and 43
Drinking straw
Chocolate coins

1 Cut the miniature swiss roll to 7.5cm (3in) long. Cover with sugarpaste and decorate as shown to form the drum.

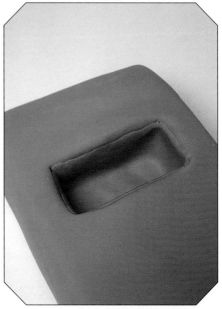

2 Cut the sponge in half lengthways and layer together. Mark the position for the drum and hollow out. Cover the whole sponge with sugarpaste.

3 Fix the drum in position. Make and fix sugarpaste surround. Pipe shells as shown, with royal icing (No.43).

4 Fix the sponge to the cake board and decorate with sugarpaste cut out in various shapes. Pipe shells shown (No.43).

5 Make and fix the handle with sugarpaste and the drinking straw. Pipe shells shown (No.43). Pipe inscription of choice (No.1). Fix chocolate money to the cake-base and board.

PESKY CROWS

20.5cm square sponge (8in)
 2 required
Swiss roll
1.5k sugarpaste (3lb)
225g royal icing (8oz)
225g butter icing (8oz)
Assorted food colours

28cm square cake board (11in)
Small leaf cutter
Continuous cutter
Serrated scraper
Fine paint brush

Poppy seeds
Sesame seeds
Board edge ribbon
Birthday ribbon
Sugarpaste blossoms

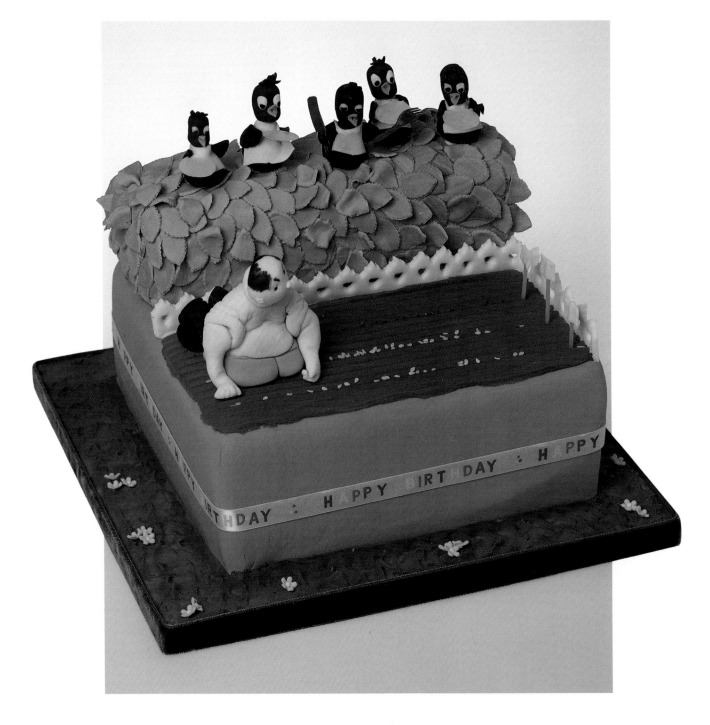

50

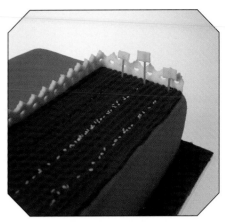

1 Coat the swiss roll with butter icing. Cut out and fix sugarpaste leaves to cover the roll as shown to form the hedge.

2 Cover the sponge with sugarpaste and fix to the board. Spread royal icing onto half the cake-top using the serrated scraper to create the grooves. Then stipple the board with royal icing.

3 Cut out and fix a sugarpaste trellis. Make and insert seed tags. Sprinkle seeds into the grooves.

4 Mould a sugarpaste crow in the sequence shown.

5 Decorate the crow with a sugarpaste bib. Make a selection of large and small crows with plates, knife and fork.

6 Mould the body and legs with sugarpaste.

7 Bend the legs as shown, then fix the body. Squash the arms to the body to create the rolled up jumper effect. Make and fix polo neck and boots.

8 Make and fix arms and head. Paint on the eyebrows and hair.

9 Fix the hedge to the cake-top then the crows in a row as shown. Fix sugarpaste blossoms around the board as required.

STRAWBERRIES and CREAM

INGREDIENTS

Sponge baked in a 1.2Lt
 pudding basin (2pt)
Small swiss roll
680g sugarpaste (1½lb)
Blue and red food colours

EQUIPMENT and DECORATIONS

30.5cm oval cake board (12in)
Decorative board covering
Piping tube
Board edge ribbon

1 Fix the decorative board covering to the board. Cover the sponge with sugarpaste. Using a piping tube, cut out circles and fill with white sugarpaste.

2 Cut the swiss roll to jug shape, then cover with sugarpaste, moulding the handle and top.

3 Mould strawberries from sugarpaste. Fresh strawberries dipped in water, then sugar can be used if eaten the same day.

4 Fix the bowl and jug to the board, then fix sugarpaste cream as shown.

HEDGIE HEDGEHOG

INGREDIENTS

15cm square sponge (6in)
 2 required
Large swiss roll
225g royal icing (8oz)
1.75k sugarpaste (3½lb)
Pink dusting powder
Assorted food colours

EQUIPMENT and DECORATIONS

35.5cm oval cake board (12in)
Cocktail stick
Paint brush
Sugar flowers
Board edge ribbon

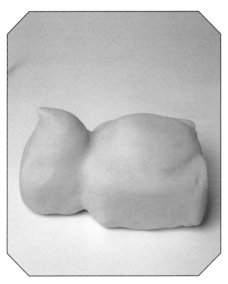

1 Using the sponges and swiss roll, fix together, then trim to the shape shown. Cover with sugarpaste.

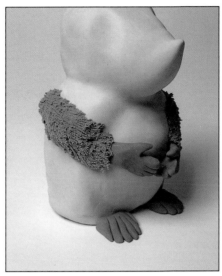

2 Place upright and cover the back with sugarpaste. Make and fix sugarpaste arms, using a cocktail stick to create prickles. Make and fix the feet.

3 Stipple the board with royal icing, then fix the cake on top. Make and fix the head of hair with sugarpaste.

4 Complete the head as shown. Brush with dusting powder.

5 Select or make a variety of sugar flowers.

6 Make and fix a sugarpaste holder for the flowers, then fill. Fix flowers over the board.

INGREDIENTS

25.5 x 20.5cm sponge (10 x 8in)
 2 required
Sponge baked in a 600ml pudding
 basin (1pt)
1.75k sugarpaste (3½lb)
115g royal icing (4oz)
Assorted food colours

EQUIPMENT and DECORATIONS

30.5 x 25.5cm cake board (12 x 10in)
Coarse cloth
Rule
Piping tube No.1
Board edge ribbon

1 Sandwich the sponges together. Roll out mottled sugarpaste and mark with the cloth, then cover the sponges in an upright position. Fix to the board. Mark lines shown. Stipple the board with royal icing.

2 Trim the pudding shaped sponge to body shape. Cover with sugarpaste. Make and fix legs and trousers, then fix the body.

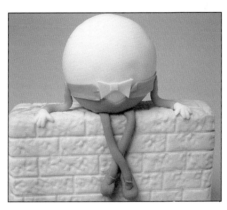

3 Cut out and fix jacket, bow tie, arms, hands and shoes.

4 Cut out and fix facial features as shown.

5 Mould sugarpaste pieces for a soldier.

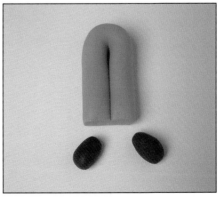

6 Mould the trousers and shoes.

7 Fix the pieces together then pipe in the eyes with royal icing. make as many as required. Fix to the board and decorate with sugarpaste drums.

VINTAGE YEAR

INGREDIENTS

Large swiss roll, 2 required
1.5k sugarpaste (3lb)
115g royal icing (4oz)
Assorted dusting powders
Assorted food colours

EQUIPMENT and DECORATIONS

35.5cm oval cake board (14in)
Decorative board covering
Crimper
Paint brush
Confectioner's varnish
Cocktail stick
Piping tube No.2
Congratulations motto

1 Fix the decorative covering to the board. Trim the swiss roll to bottle shape and cover with sugarpaste. Crimp the bottom edge of the bottle.

2 Cut out and fix sugarpaste label and cork top.

3 Fix a large cone shape piece of sugarpaste against the bottle, then start to make and fix grapes.

4 Make light and dark shades of grapes, then brush with edible confectioner's varnish. Pipe the lines shown with royal icing (No.2).

5 Cut out a variety of sugarpaste vine leaves and colour with dusting powders.

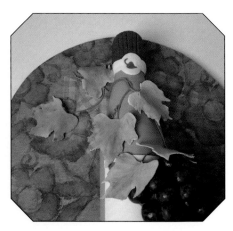

6 Fix the leaves to the lines, then decorate the cake and board as required.

INGREDIENTS

20.5cm square sponge (8in)
2 required
1.25k sugarpaste (2½lb)
225g royal icing (8oz)
Assorted food colours

EQUIPMENT and DECORATIONS

28cm square cake board (11in)
Decorative board covering
Piping tubes No.1 and 43
Paint brush
Candles and holders

1 Fix the covering to the board. Layer the sponges together, then cut out a 'V' from either side. Cover with sugarpaste.

2 Fix the cake to the board as shown. Pipe shells along the edges and rope for the handle with royal icing (No.43).

3 Cut out and fix a selection of sugarpaste characters to the cake-top, then pipe the lines as shown (No.1).

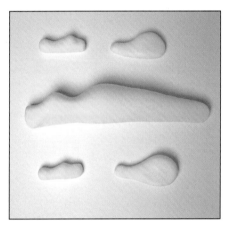

4 Mould the various shapes shown using sugarpaste.

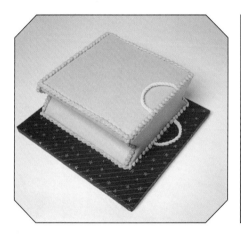

5 Fix the pieces together to form the character shown.

6 Repeat steps four and five to create the character shown.

7 Repeat steps four and five to create the character shown. Pipe inscription of choice onto the cake-top (No.1).

GOLF BAG

INGREDIENTS

25.5cm square sponge (10in)
15cm square sponge (6in)
1.5k sugarpaste (3lb)
225g royal icing (8oz)
Assorted food colours

EQUIPMENT and DECORATIONS

51 x 28cm oblong cake board
 (20 x11in)
Crimper
Marker
Piping tube No.2
Board edge ribbon

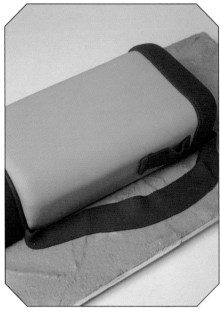

1 Trim the sponges and cover with sugarpaste to form the bag shape. Fix to the board, then stipple the remaining board surface with royal icing.

2 Make and fix sugarpaste strap and edging.

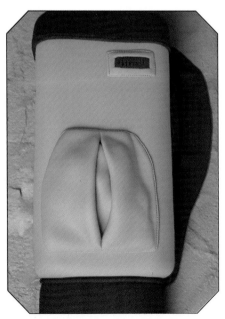

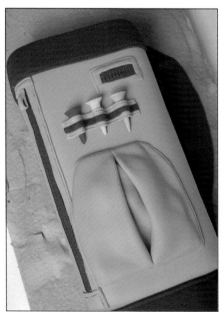

3 Make and fix sugarpaste pockets.

4 Make and fix zip and tees.

5 Make and fix sugarpaste clubs and putter. Decorate with golf ball and inscription of choice.

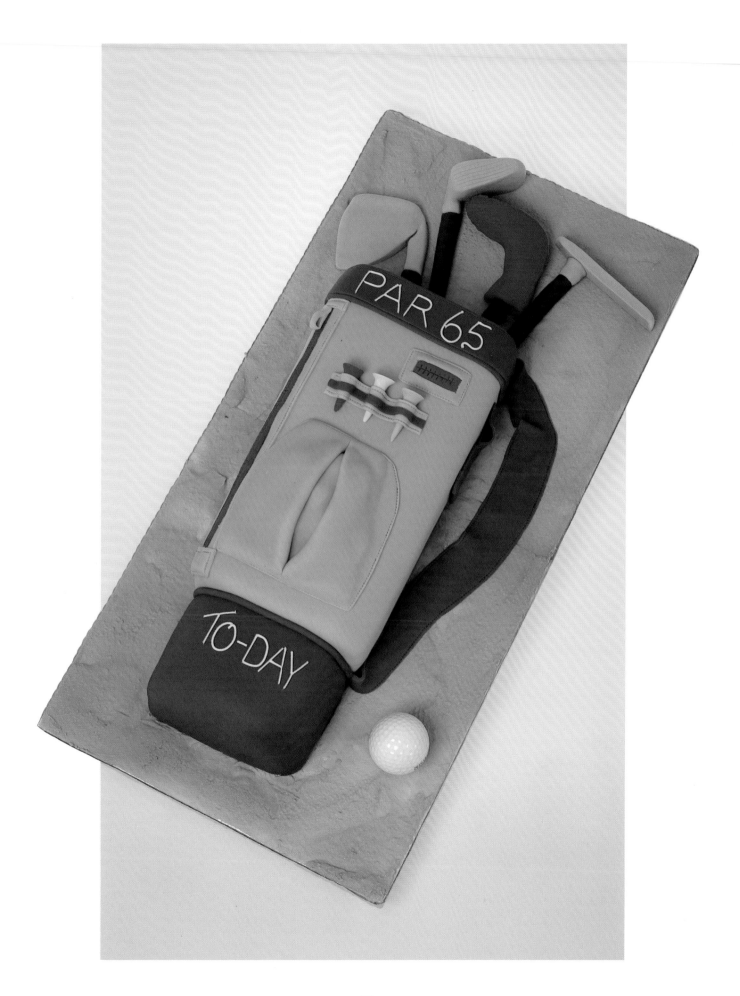

20.5cm hexagonal sponge (8in)
 2 required
10, 13 and 15cm round sponges
 (4, 5 and 6in) 2 of each size required
Sponge baked in a 900ml pudding
 basin (1½pt)
1.5k sugarpaste (3lb)
225g royal icing (8oz)

35.5 and 30.5cm hexagonal cake boards
 (14 and 12in)
15cm round cake card (6in)
Piping tube No.7
Scalloped cutter
Decorative thick card
Dowel
Blossoms
Board edge ribbon

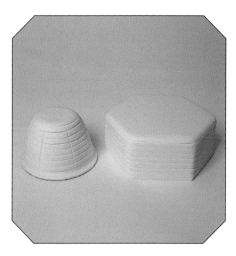

1 Layer the large sponges together and cover with sugarpaste. Mark the lines shown. Cover the pudding shaped sponge with sugarpaste and mark the lines.

2 Fix to the board then stipple with royal icing. Pipe shells around the base (No.7). Cut out and fix sugarpaste windows and doors.

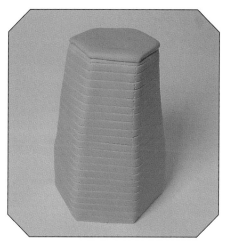

3 Layer the remaining hexagonal sponges together, trim to angle shown, then cover with sugarpaste and mark the lines.

4 Fix to the cake-top. Pipe shells around the base (No.7). Decorate with cut-out sugarpaste windows.

5 Place the top onto small card and fix to the cake-top. Decorate with cut out sugarpaste pieces. Insert a length of dowel.

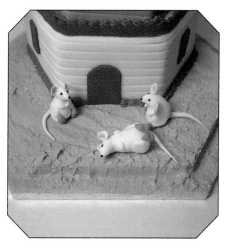

6 Make and decorate sugarpaste mice as shown. Cut out card and fix to the dowel for the sails.

PUSSY CATS

INGREDIENTS

Large swiss roll, 2 required
1.75k sugarpaste (3½lb)
115g royal icing (4oz)
Assorted food colours

1 Fix the decorative covering to the board. Cut a piece off swiss roll and place in the position shown. Trim to cat shape.

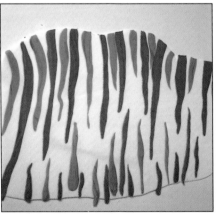

2 Roll out sugarpaste to oblong shape, then fix various lengths of coloured sugarpaste as shown. Roll out to even thickness.

3 Fix over the sponge and press firmly to pronounce the shape.

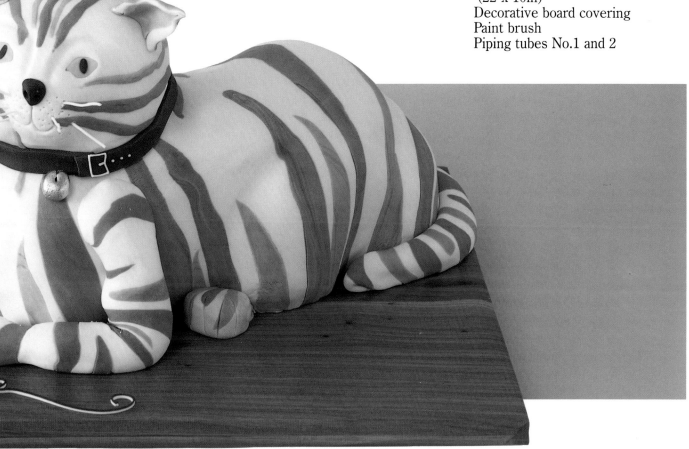

56 x 25.5cm oblong cake board
 (22 x 10in)
Decorative board covering
Paint brush
Piping tubes No.1 and 2

4 Make and fix the ears, eyes and nose. Mark the mouth as shown.

5 Mould and fix the front legs, back paws and tail.

6 Make and fix collar, bell and whiskers. Repeat for second cat and fix to the board.
Pipe inscription with royal icing (No.2 and 1).

U.F.O.

INGREDIENTS

20.5cm round sponge (8in)
 3 required
1.5k sugarpaste (3lb)
115g royal icing (4oz)
Assorted food colours

EQUIPMENT and DECORATIONS

40.5cm round cake board (16in)
Fine paint brush
2 drinking straws
Piping tube No.1
Board edge ribbon

1 Cut thick circles of sugarpaste and press in the centres whilst pinching up the sides to create craters. 5 required.

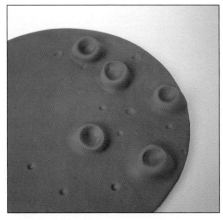

2 Fix the craters to the board and carefully cover with a thin layer of sugarpaste, keeping the shape of the craters. Press dimples into the paste, using the end of a paint brush.

3 Layer the three sponges together with filling of choice. Trim the sides to the shape shown. Coat with butter icing then chill before covering with sugarpaste.

4 Cut out and fix sugarpaste windows, door and rim. Then fix to the board. Insert two drinking straws with sugarpaste tops as shown in main picture.

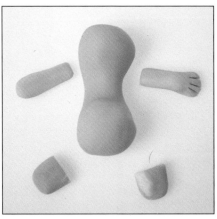

5 Mould the various parts with sugarpaste for a body.

6 Fix the pieces together. Make and fix ears and eyes. 6 various sizes and shapes required. Place on cake board. Pipe inscription of choice with royal icing (No.1).

PLUMBER'S MATE

INGREDIENTS

20.5cm square sponge (8in)
 2 required
Small swiss roll
Cake card
1.25k sugarpaste (2½lb)
Assorted food colours

EQUIPMENT and DECORATIONS

35.5 x 25.5cm oblong shaped cake board
Decorative board covering
Flag

1 Fix the decorative covering to the board. Layer the sponges together, place on end and cover with sugarpaste as shown. Fix to a piece of cake card then to the board.

2 Cut out and fix mottled sugarpaste doors and handles.

3 Cut cake card to match the large door, and cover with mottled sugarpaste. Leave to dry.

4 Cut and shape the swiss roll to form body shape, then cover with sugarpaste as shown.

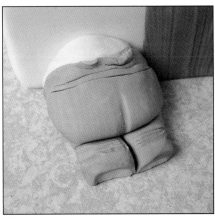

5 Fix to a piece of cake card, then to the board with sugarpaste for the body back.

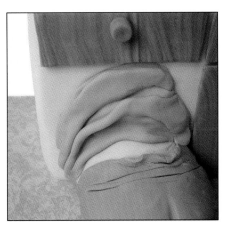

6 Make and fix sugarpaste crumpled shirt.

7 Make and fix sugarpaste shoes.

8 Make and fix sugarpaste taps and hand. Write message of choice onto the flag and fix to the hand.

9 Make a selection of sugarpaste tools and plumbing fittings. Fix the door in position.

CACTUS

INGREDIENTS

Sponge baked in a 1.2Lt pudding
 basin (2pt)
Small sponge cakes
1.5k sugarpaste (3lb)
Wheat cereal biscuits
115g royal icing (4oz)
60g Modelling paste (2oz)
Green, red and orange food
 colouring

EQUIPMENT and DECORATIONS

20.5, 23, 25.5 and 28cm round cake
 boards (8, 9, 10 and 11in)
Cocktail stick
Modelling tool
Embosser
Piping tube No.1
Round crimped cutter
Card

Fix the boards together using either royal icing without glycerin, glue or double-sided sellotape. Avoid pins as they may cause injury.

1 Fix the cake boards together as shown.

2 Roll out and fix sugarpaste to the three board edges, as shown.

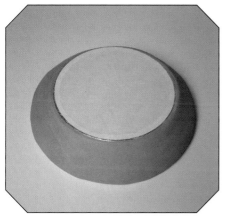

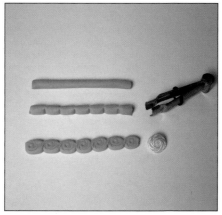

3 Cover the side with sugarpaste to form the bowl shape.

4 Roll out a length of sugarpaste, crimp and then emboss to form design shown.

5 Upturn the bowl and fix the edging. Crumb sufficient wheat cereal biscuits to fill the top.

6 Cover the sponges with sugarpaste and press down the sides with a modelling tool, to form the cactus shape. Place the large cactus onto the bowl.

7 Make small holes in the cake-side and insert short lengths of moulded modelling paste. Repeat with small sponges to form miniature cacti.

8 Cut out and frill crimped circles of sugarpaste to form the flower. Pipe the pollen with royal icing. Pipe inscription of choice onto card.

20.5cm round sponge (8in)
 2 required
680g sugarpaste (1½lb)
115g modelling paste (4oz)
Dessicated coconut
Assorted food colours

28cm round cake board (11in)
Fine paint brush
Clown candles
Board edge ribbon

1 Cover the cake and board with sugarpaste. Cut and fix a sugarpaste rim. Spread a little butter icing onto the cake-top and board then sprinkle with coloured dessicated coconut.

2 Using the templates as a guide, cut out the pieces shown from thinly rolled modelling paste and leave until dry.

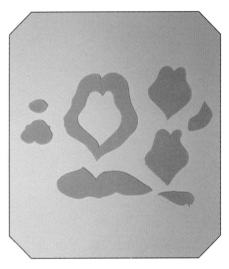

3 Cut out the further pieces shown and leave until dry.

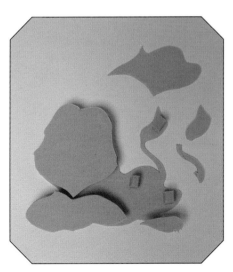

4 When dry assemble the pieces as shown, using small blocks of modelling paste to raise the layers.

5 Fix the final pieces, then paint in the features as shown.

6 Repeat steps 2 to 4 for the seals, balls and centre stand. Fix to the cake then fix the candles as required.

SEWING BOX

INGREDIENTS

20.5 x 15cm oblong sponge
 (8 x 6in) 2 required
900g sugarpaste (2lb)
225g royal icing (8oz)
Assorted food colours

EQUIPMENT and DECORATIONS

28cm square cake board (11in)
20.5 x 15cm oblong cake card
 (8 x 6in)
Decorative board covering
Cocktail stick
Paint brush

Embosser
Crimper
Piping tube No.43
Dowel
Plaque

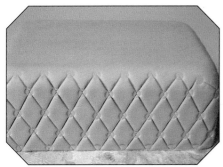

1 Fix the decorative covering to the board. Layer the sponges together and cover with sugarpaste. Mark the lines, then emboss at the centres.

2 Crimp lengths of sugarpaste and then emboss. Fix to the cake-top as shown.

3 Make and fix sewing items from sugarpaste. Sugarpaste the card, then pipe shells along the edge with royal icing (No.43). Support with dowel as shown in main picture.

FISH PLATTER

INGREDIENTS

23cm round sponge (9in)
900g sugarpaste (2lb)
115g royal icing (4oz)
Assorted dusting powders
Assorted food colours

EQUIPMENT and DECORATIONS

35.5cm oval cake board (14in)
Medium paint brush
Piping tube No.2
Lemon and parsley
Board edge ribbon

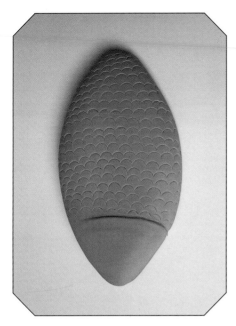

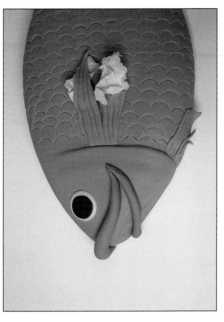

1 Using the template as a guide, trim the sponge to fish shape and cover with sugarpaste. Mark the scales with the wide end of a piping tube. Make and fix the gills.

2 Make and fix the mouth and eye. Cut out a fin and fix to the cake, supporting with tissue paper until dry.

3 Cut out and fix additional fins and a tail. Mark with the back of a knife.

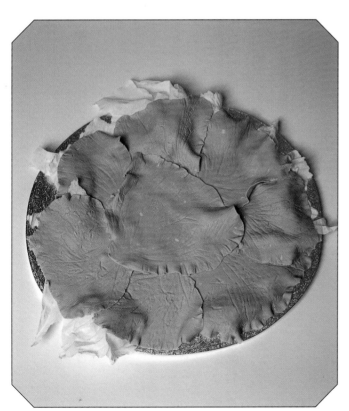

4 Cut out and fix various size sugarpaste lettuce leaves to the cake board. Support with tissue paper until dry.

5 Brush the fish with dusting powders, then fix onto the leaves. Decorate as required.

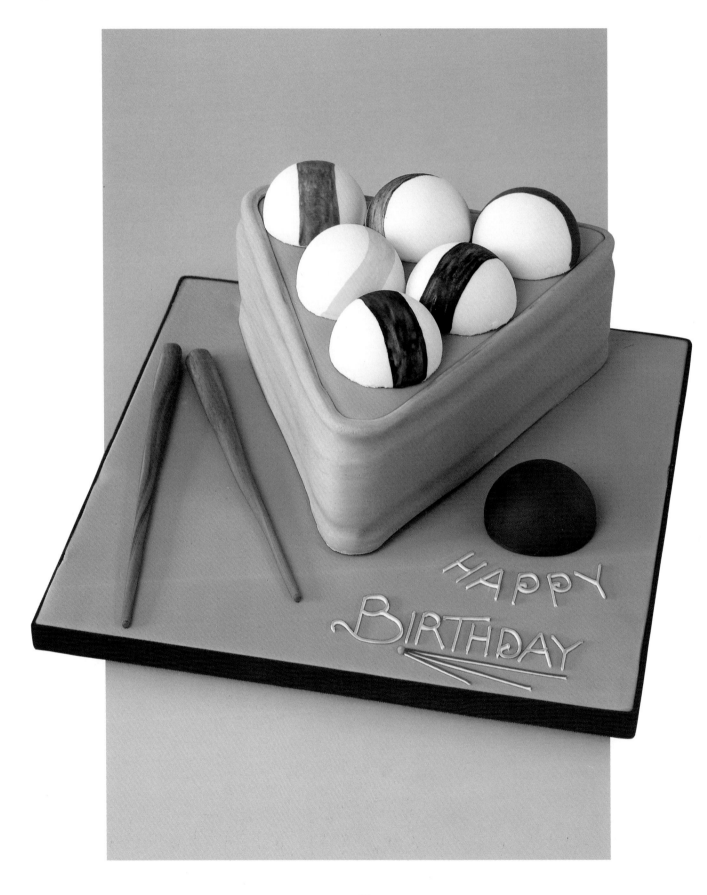

20.5cm square sponge (8in)
 2 required
1.5k sugarpaste (3lb)
60g modelling paste (2oz)
115g royal icing (4oz)
Assorted food colours

30.5cm square cake board (12in)
Ice-cream scoop
Paint brush
Piping tubes No.1 and 2
Board edge ribbon

1 Layer the sponges together, then trim to shape. Cover with two colours of sugarpaste.

2 Mix 225g (8oz) of sugarpaste with the flower paste. Press paste into the scoop.

3 Trim the edge, then gently turn out.

4 Make a selection of half-balls colouring lines at various angles, as shown.

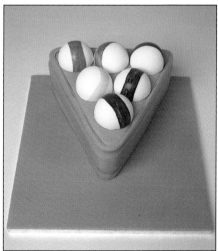

5 Cover the board with sugarpaste, then fix the cake and balls.

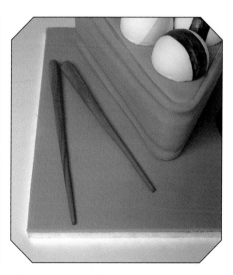

6 Make sugarpaste cues and fix to the board. Pipe inscription of choice with royal icing (No.2 and 1).

Sponge baked in a 1.2Lt
  pudding basin (2pt)
Sponge baked in a 600ml
  pudding basin (1pt)

1.5k sugarpaste (3lb)
225g royal icing (8oz)
Red dusting powder
Assorted food colours

38cm round cake board (15in)
Fine paint brush
Board edge ribbon

1 Stipple the board with royal icing to form the sea. Trim the small sponge to round ball shape for the head. Cover the sponges with sugarpaste.

2 Roll out sugarpaste in two colours, then cut out the pieces shown for the swimsuit top.

3 Fix the swimsuit to the large sponge. Then fix to the coated board.

4 Make and fix sugarpaste eyes, nose, mouth and ears to the small sponge. Fix to the body.

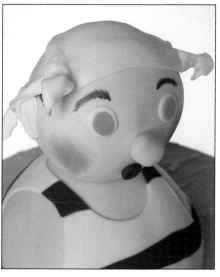

5 Brush dusting powder for the cheeks. Paint on the eyebrows and hair. Make and fix a sugarpaste knotted handkerchief.

6 Make and fix a sugarpaste rubber ring, then the arms as shown.

RUCKSACK and BOOTS

INGREDIENTS

25.5cm square sponge (10in)
 2 required
1.5k sugarpaste (3lb)
115g royal icing (4oz)
Assorted food colours

EQUIPMENT and DECORATIONS

45.5cm x 30.5cm oblong cake
 board (16 x 12in)
Decorative board covering
Cake card
Piping tubes No.1 and 7

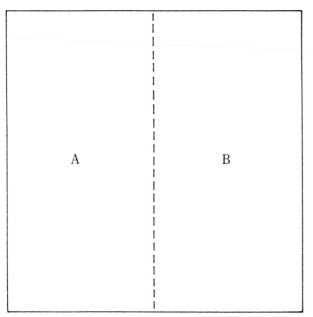

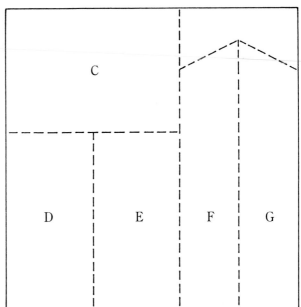

25.5cm (10in) Square Cakes

1 Cover board with decorative paper. Cut A and B cake shapes, layer and cover with sugarpaste. Fix to card cut to size. Cut, layer and cover D and E. Fix to card. Fix cakes to the board.

2 Cut and cover F and G. Fix to card then to the board. Pipe shells along the edges with royal icing (No.7).

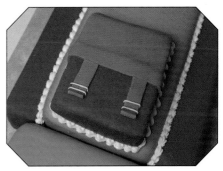

3 Cut and cover C with sugarpaste and fix to the cake-top. Cut and fix sugarpaste top and straps. Pipe shells as shown (No.7). Pipe the lines (No.1).

4 Cut and fix sugarpaste tops and straps shown. Pipe the lines (No.1).

5 Cut and fix the sugarpaste straps and lace then pipe the lines (No.1).

6 Make a pair of sugarpaste walking boots. Pipe the laces (No.1). Pipe the inscription of choice onto a sugarpaste tag (No.1).

20.5cm square sponges (8in)
 3 required
Sponge baked in a 300ml
 pudding basin (½pt)
1.75k sugarpaste (3½lb)
Assorted food colours

35.5cm square cake board (14in)
Decorative board covering
Crimper
Modelling tools
Numerals

1 Fix the covering to the board. Cut the sponge to shape shown, then cover with sugarpaste.

2 Using sugarpaste, cut out and fix the clock face crimping the edge. Make and fix the hands, then fix the numerals.

3 Decorate the clock edges with crimped sugarpaste and cut-outs.

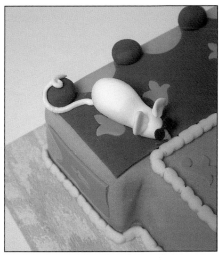

4 Cut out and fix sugarpaste crown. Make and fix baubles.

5 Mould and fix a sugarpaste mouse, as shown. 3 required.

6 Trim the basin shaped sponge and cover with sugarpaste to make the cat. Position on board as shown.

COUNT DRACULA

INGREDIENTS

30.5cm square sponge (12in)
Swiss roll
1.5k sugarpaste (3lb)
115g royal icing (4oz)

EQUIPMENT and DECORATIONS

35.5 x 25.5cm oblong cake board
 (14 x 10in)
Decorative board covering
Paint brush
Modelling tool
Dowel
Piping tube No.1

Increase the template to match the size of the cake being used.

1 Fix the covering to the board. Cut the sponge down the middle, layer, then trim to coffin shape and cover with sugarpaste.

2 Roll out a sheet of sugarpaste, ruffle to resemble silk and fix to the cake-top.

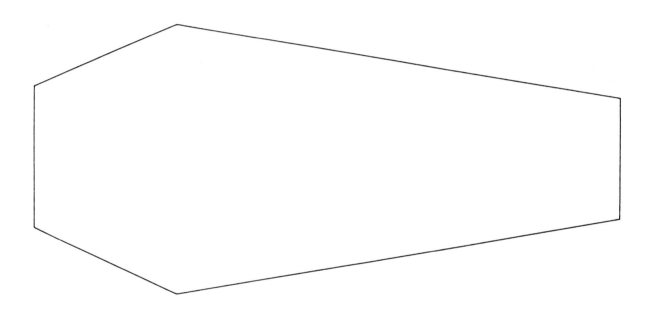

3 Cut the swiss roll in half, then cover with sugarpaste, moulding to head shape. Cut out and fix ears.

4 Fix to the cake-top, using dowel for support. Pipe the hair, then paint the eyes. Make and fix the mouth and teeth.

5 Cut out and fix the sugarpaste cloak and hand. Using the remaining swiss roll, make and decorate pot with dentures. Pipe inscription of choice (No.1).

WEDDING TOPPERS

INGREDIENTS

15cm round cake (6in)
 2 required
900g almond paste (2lb)
Sponge baked in a 1.2Lt
 pudding basin (2pt)
Black and apricot food colours

EQUIPMENT and DECORATIONS

30.5cm round cake board (12in)
25.5cm round cake board (10in)
Crimped cutters
Cocktail stick
Flowers
Board edge ribbon

1 Cover the sponge and large board with sugarpaste, pressing around the base, to form the bride's hat.

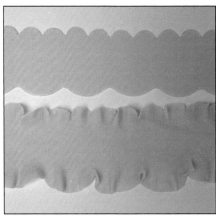

2 Roll out a length of sugarpaste, cut narrow and wide curves with cutters. Immediately frill the edges with a cocktail stick.

3 Fix the frill around the cake base, then make and fix a second frill. Cut and fix sugarpaste ribbon shaped ends then fix flowers of choice.

4 Cover the remaining board with sugarpaste. Layer the cakes together with almond paste then cover with sugarpaste and fix to the board.

5 Using the template as a guide, roll out and cut a sugarpaste glove.

6 Immediately fix the glove to the hat then cut and fix a second glove. Cut and fix a sugarpaste band around the base. Fix flower of choice and then ribbon around the board edge.

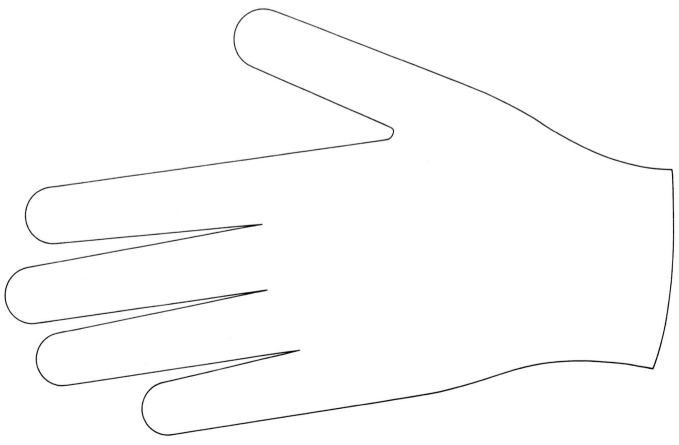

NOAH'S ARK

INGREDIENTS

25.5cm square sponge (10in)
15cm square sponge (6in)
1.5k sugarpaste (3lb)
450g modelling paste (1lb)
225g royal icing (8oz)
Assorted food colours

EQUIPMENT and DECORATIONS

35.5 x 30.5cm oblong cake board
 (14 x 12in)
Paint brush
Piping tube No.1
Card
Extended cutter
Board edge ribbon

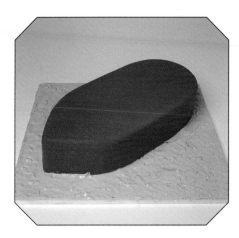

1 Using the template as a guide, cut the large sponge in half and layer. Then trim to hull shape. Cover with sugarpaste and place onto the board. Stipple the board with royal icing.

2 Cut and layer the remaining sponge to cabin shape. Cover with sugarpaste. Cut and fix a decorative strip of sugarpaste around the base.

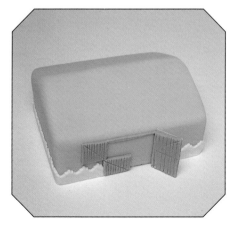

3 Cut out and fix sugarpaste doors and windows.

Increase the template to match the size of the cake being used.

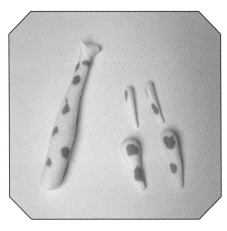

4 Insert small brown-coloured pieces of modelling paste into main colour. Mould paste into the shapes shown.

5 Fix the pieces together to form a giraffe. Two required. Pipe the eyes with royal icing (No.1).

6 Mould the shapes shown for pigs.

7 Fix the pieces together to form the pig. Two required. Pipe the eyes with royal icing (No.1).

8 Mould the shapes shown for rabbits.

9 Fix the pieces together to form a rabbit. Two required. Pipe the eyes and noses with royal icing (No.1).

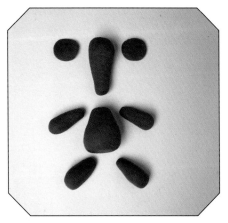

10 Mould the shapes shown for elephants.

11 Fix the pieces together to form an elephant. Two required. Pipe the eyes with royal icing (No.1).

12 Make and fix a modelling paste ramp, using card for support. Make and fix modelling paste snakes. Fix the animals as required, making a few more if necessary.

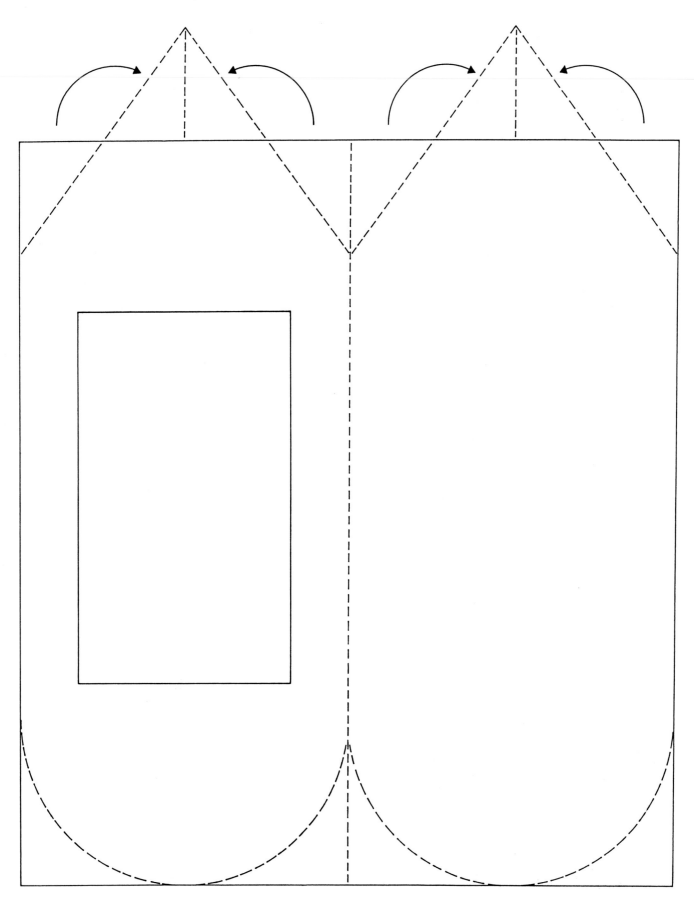

Increase the template to
match the size of the
cake being used.

DUSTY BIN

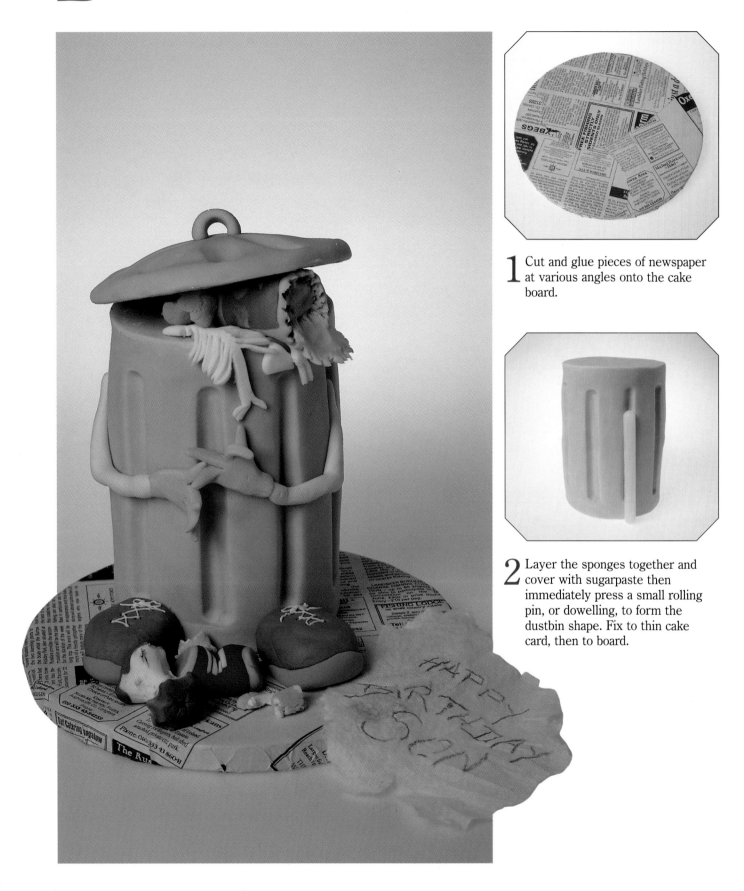

1 Cut and glue pieces of newspaper at various angles onto the cake board.

2 Layer the sponges together and cover with sugarpaste then immediately press a small rolling pin, or dowelling, to form the dustbin shape. Fix to thin cake card, then to board.

INGREDIENTS

13cm round sponge cake (5in)
 6 required
900g sugarpaste (2lb)
115g royal icing (4oz)
Assorted food colours

EQUIPMENT and DECORATIONS

23cm round cake board (9in)
13cm round cake card (5in)
 2 required
Piping tube No.1
Fine paint brush
Board covering of choice
Small rolling pin or dowel

3 Mould sugarpaste onto the remaining cake card, indent to form lid pattern then make and fix a handle. Leave to dry.

4 Make and fix sugarpaste shoes, then pipe laces as shown, with royal icing (No.1).

5 Mould and fix two strips for the arms, then make and fix glove covered hands.

6 Make a selection of sugarpaste rubbish for the dustbin.

7 Fix some of the sugarpaste rubbish onto the cake-top then fix the lid as shown.

8 Scatter sugarpaste rubbish onto the cake board. Write message of choice with a pen onto tissue paper, crumple then fix to the board.

INGREDIENTS

25.5cm square cake (10in)
25.5cm round cake (10in)
15cm square cake (6in) 2 required
3.5k almond paste (7lb)
4.5k sugarpaste (9lb)
115g modelling paste (4oz)
115g royal icing (4oz)
Pink and lilac food colours

EQUIPMENT and DECORATIONS

40.5cm square cake board (16in)
25.5cm round cake card (10in)
15cm square cake card (6in)
 2 required
Small stiff paint brush
Piping tube No.42
Floral wire
Plastic doves
Dowel
Various ribbons
Board edge ribbon

1 Sugarpaste the board, then stipple with colouring. Cover the large cake with sugarpaste, mark the sides then fix ribbons and cake to the board.

2 Cover the round cake with sugarpaste, cutting out sections and in-filling with another colour.

3 Make and fix a sugarpaste lid. Fix ribbons, then fix to the cake card.

4 Layer the small square cakes together, then cover with sugarpaste. Cut out circles and fill with another colour. Fix to the cake card.

5 Cut the remaining cake card from point to point and cover each side with sugarpaste. Fix to the cake-top supporting until dry. Pipe shells with royal icing (No.42).

6 Wrap narrow strips of modelling paste around dowel and slide off to dry, creating curls.

7 Roll out a thin sheet of sugarpaste, ruffle and fix to the cake-top. Fix doves to floral wire and insert as shown. Decorate the cake as required.

LUCKY HORSESHOE

INGREDIENTS

25.5cm horseshoe shaped cake
 (25.5cm)
1.25k almond paste (2½lb)
1.25k sugarpaste (2½lb)
340g royal icing (12oz)
Assorted food colours

EQUIPMENT and DECORATIONS

38cm round cake board (15in)
Piping tubes No.2 and 43
Crimper
Paint brush
Board edge ribbon

1 Cover the cake with almond paste, then sugarpaste. Place onto the board, then stipple the remaining board surface with royal icing.

2 Cut out and fix sugarpaste top. Crimp the edge, then cut out nail holes. Using the template as a guide, cut out sugarpaste horses.

3 Paint the eyes, noses and manes. Fix to the cake-side, then pipe the reins (No.2). Pipe shells around the base (No.43).

4 Make and fix sugarpaste stirrups between the horses.

5 Make and fix a selection of sugarpaste clothing. Pipe inscription of choice (No.2).

INGREDIENTS

25.5cm square sponge (10in)
 2 required
Miniature swiss roll, 4 required
1.5k sugarpaste (3lb)
115g royal icing (4oz)
Assorted food colours

EQUIPMENT and DECORATIONS

40.5 x 35.5cm oblong cake board
 (16 x 14in)
25.5 x 13cm cake card (10 x 5in)
Decorative board covering
Miniature cutters
Piping tubes No.1, 2 and 42
Dowel
Board edge ribbon
Indoor sparklers

1 Fix the covering to the board. Cut the sponges in half, then layer three pieces together and cover with sugarpaste making a raised edge around the top.

2 Pipe shells around the base with royal icing (No.42). Make and fix sugarpaste fireworks around the cake-side.

3 Cover the remaining sponge with sugarpaste and fix to the card. Cut out the letters shown in sugarpaste. Pipe shells around the base (No.42).

4 Cover a swiss roll with sugarpaste and make the rocket as shown. Insert dowel for stick.

5 Using the remaining swiss rolls to make a selection of fireworks. Cut out and fix sugarpaste miniature stars. Fix sparklers.

BOW TIE and TAILS

INGREDIENTS

25.5 x 18cm oblong sponge
 (10 x 7in)
1.75k sugarpaste (3½lb)
115g royal icing (4oz)
Assorted food colours

EQUIPMENT and DECORATIONS

40.5 x 23cm oblong cake board
 (16 x 9in)
Decorative board covering
Frill cutter
Cocktail stick

Crimped round cutter
Crimper
Embosser
Piping tube No.1
Asparagus fern

1 Fix the covering to the board. Cover the sponge with sugarpaste. Cut out, frill, then fix sugarpaste portion of shirt shown.

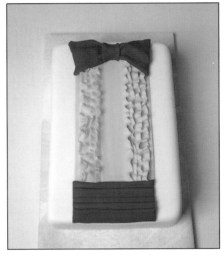

2 Make and fix sugarpaste bow tie and fluted cummerbund.

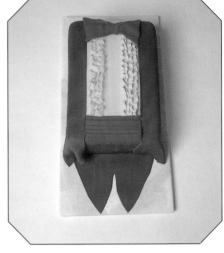

3 Cover the sides to create the jacket with tails.

4 Cut out and fix the lapels, then crimp the edges.

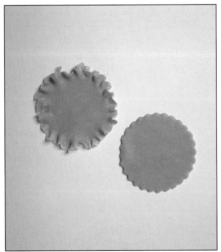

5 Cut out crimped discs of sugarpaste, then frill the edges with a cocktail stick. Layer together to form a carnation.

6 Fix the carnation and fern to the lapel, then make and fix embossed sugarpaste buttons. Pipe inscription of choice with royal icing (No.1).

SING-A-SONG OF SIXPENCE

INGREDIENTS

23cm hexagonal cake (9in)
900g almond paste (2lb)
1.5k sugarpaste (3lb)
225g royal icing (8oz)
115g modelling paste (4oz)
Assorted dusting powders
Assorted food colours

EQUIPMENT and DECORATIONS

35.5cm petal shaped cake board (14in)
Piping tubes No.1 and 43
Fine paint brushes
Edible pens
Cocktail stick
Candles and holders
Small quantity of rice
Board edge ribbon

1 Cover the cake and board with sugarpaste. Allow to dry thoroughly. Paint each petal of board in the manner shown. Draw, then paint in the picture shown. Repeat picture opposite side.

2 Draw, then paint in the maid. Paint cloud background, grass, washing line and clothes basket. Repeat picture opposite side.

3 Draw, then paint the Queen in her parlour. Paint the curtains, then draw in the window panes. Repeat picture opposite side.

4 Using modelling paste, cut out table and legs. Assemble and support until dry. Make pots of money and individual coins. Fix to table and floor.

5 Using modelling paste, cut out the washing and fix on line, supporting until dry. Make and fix blackbird.

6 Make a modelling paste table. Cut out and frill a table cloth to fit over the table. Make and fix bread and honey.

 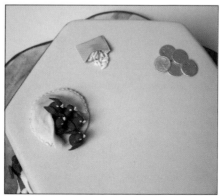 

7 Mould a pie and small birds. Assemble as shown. Fix on cake-top.

8 Press coins into sugarpaste, cut out and paint silver. Make a small sugarpaste purse and fill with rice as shown. Fix to the cake-top.

9 Pipe shells around the cake-top edge (No.43). Pipe inscription of choice (No.1). Make and fix songsheet as required.

FISHING CREEL

INGREDIENTS

20.5cm square sponge (8in)
Sponge baked in a 600ml
 pudding basin (1pt)
Swiss rolls, 2 required

1.5k sugarpaste (3lb)
340g royal icing (12oz)
Red and yellow dusting powder
Assorted food colours

EQUIPMENT and DECORATIONS

35.5cm oval cake board (14in)
Crimper
Small paint brushes
Piping tube No.1
Board edge ribbon

1 Cut the sponge to oblong shape, then cover with sugarpaste. Brush with royal icing to form grass effect.

2 Fix to the cake board. Cover remaining board surface with sugarpaste and stippled royal icing, to form bank and water.

3 Cover the pudding shaped sponge with sugarpaste and crimp to form basket weave.

4 Twist and fix lengths of sugarpaste to the basket, as shown.

5 Cut the swiss rolls in half and at different lengths. Cover roughly with sugarpaste.

6 Brush with food colours to form logs.

7 Fix the basket and logs to the sponge as shown.

8 Make and fix a sugarpaste fisherman's hat. Then decorate with sugarpaste insects.

9 Make a selection of sugarpaste fishes and rod. Pipe inscription of choice onto the water (No.1).

KING KONG

INGREDIENTS

Sponge baked in a 1.2Lt
  pudding basin (2pt)
Sponge baked in a 600ml
  pudding basin (1pt)
1.75k sugarpaste (3½lb)
Assorted food colours

EQUIPMENT and DECORATIONS

30.5cm round cake board (12in)
Leaf cutters
Modelling tools
  Fine paint brush
    Board edge ribbon

110

1 Cover the board with mottled sugarpaste. Cut out and fix sugarpaste leaves around the board.

2 Cut the two sponges to form the body and head, then cover with sugarpaste.

3 Fix darker sugarpaste to the head and mould the features shown, using modelling tools.

4 Make and fix the ears and eyes. Paint the pupils with food colouring.

5 Mould and fix sugarpaste chest to the body, then fix the head.

6 Mould sugarpaste arms and legs.

7 Fix the body to the board, then fix the legs in a sitting position. Fix the arms in a cradling position.

8 Make and fix the legs and then the body of the girl in the hands.

9 Make and fix arms and head. Decorate with a little royal icing for the hair and paint in the features.

THE THREE LITTLE PIGS

INGREDIENTS

20.5cm square sponge (8in)
 2 required
1.25k sugarpaste (2½lb)
225g modelling paste (8oz)
225g royal icing (8oz)
Assorted food colours

EQUIPMENT and DECORATIONS

35.5cm petal shaped cake board (14in)
Cocktail stick
Edible food colour pen
Small heart cutter
Piping tube No.1
Blossoms
Board edge ribbon

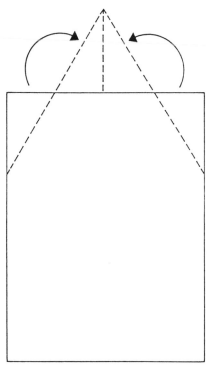

Increase the template to
match the size of the
cake being used.

1 Cover the board with sugarpaste.
Using the template as a guide, trim
the sponges to form the cottage
shape and cover with sugarpaste.
Fix to the board.

2 Cut out and fix strips of sugarpaste
for the frame work. Using an edible
pen, draw the window lines.

3 Make and fix sugarpaste door and
top window. Cover with sugarpaste,
then mark with a cocktail stick to
create thatch effect.

4 Cover the roof with sugarpaste,
then mark with the cocktail stick.
Make and fix a chimney pot.

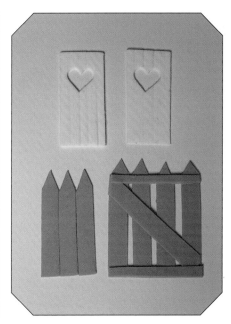

5 Cut out eight window shutters and
a gate with fencing from modelling
paste. Leave until dry.

6 When dry, fix the shutters and then pipe flora over and around the front door with royal icing. Decorate the door as required.

7 Fix the fencing in a disorderly manner, as shown.

8 Mould the various parts of a wolf with sugarpaste.

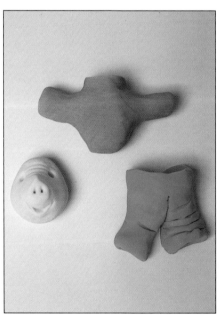

9 Fix the pieces together and mark with a cocktail stick to create fur. Paint the facial features and fur with food colouring.

10 Mould a head, jumper and trousers with sugarpaste as shown.

11 Fix the pieces together. Make and fix hands, feet and ears. Three pigs required in various positions. Fix to the board and decorate with blossoms.

CHRISTMAS GOODIES

INGREDIENTS

18cm round sponge (7in)
 2 required
680g sugarpaste (1½lb)
115g royal icing (4oz)
Red, brown and green food
 colours

EQUIPMENT and DECORATIONS

30.5cm round cake board (12in)
Crimper
Rule
Tissue paper
Holy cutter

Extended cutter
Piping tube No.1
Assorted sweets and
 chocolates

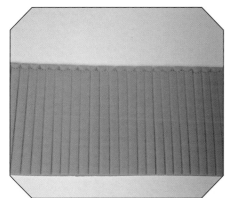

1 Sandwich the sponges together. Roll out sugarpaste to twice the height of the cake. Mark even lines with a rule then crimp the top edge.

2 Fix around the cake then support with tissue paper to form the shape of an open sack. Cut and fix a sugarpaste band around the cake-base.

3 Roll out and fix sugarpaste ties, then cut out and fix label and holly. Pipe message of choice with royal icing (No.1). Remove the tissue paper when dry and fill with sweets.

20.5cm square cake (8in)
900g almond paste (2lb)
1.5k sugarpaste (3lb)
170g royal icing (6oz)
Assorted food colours

30.5cm square cake board (12in)
Crimped cutter
Rule
Piping tube No.1
Seasonal decorations
Board edge ribbon

1 Fix the covering to the board. Cut the cake to house shape and cover with almond paste, then sugarpaste.

2 Mark the sides with a rule. Cut out decorative strips of sugarpaste and start the roof.

3 Finish the roof, then make and fix a sugarpaste chimney.

4 Make and fix a sugarpaste hand holding a bag.

5 Make a selection of sugarpaste figures and toys.

6 Stipple the house with royal icing to resemble snow. Fix the sugarpaste figures and toys. Pipe inscription of choice (No.1), then decorate as required.

INDEX AND GLOSSARY

A

Abbreviations
cm	– centimetre	
°C	– degrees centigrade	
°F	– degrees farenheit	
dsp	– dessertspoon	
g	– gram	
hrs	– hours	
in	– inch	
lbs	– pounds	
k	– kilo	
oz	– ounces	
Lt	– litre	
mins	– minutes	
ml	– millilitre	
(No.)	– piping tube number	
pt	– pint	
tsp	– teaspoon	
tbsp	– tablespoon	

ALL AT SEA cake	82
All-in-one Fruit cake	14
All-in-one Sponge cake	10
All-in-one Swiss Roll	16
Almond Paste	18
Animals	94
Author	3

B

BIG BREAKFAST cake	32
BILLIARDS cake	80
BIRTHDAY ELEPHANT cake	30
BIRTHDAY GALLEON cake	41
Boots	85
BOW TIE an1d TAILS cake	104
Butter icing	19

C

CACTUS cake	72

Cake-base: Where the bottom edges of the cake meet the cake board

CAKE BOXES cake	98

Cake-card: A thin cake card

CHRISTMAS CALLER cake	116
CHRISTMAS GOODIES cake	115
CIRCUS TIME cake	74
Colouring and painting	18
– sugarpaste	20

Contents	4
COUNT DRACULA cake	88
Covering cakes	20
Crow	51

D

Decorative board covering	23
DUSTY BIN cake	96

E

Elephant	30
Equipment	22

F

FATHER'S DAY cake	46
Female figure	45
FIREWORKS cake	102
FISH PLATTER cake	78
FISHING BOAT cake	26
FISHING CREEL cake	108
Fixing	23

Frills: To make frills, place tapered end of a cocktail stick, or paintbrush handle, over the edge of thinly rolled sugarpaste and rock it back and forth a little at a time.

G

GOLF BAG cake	62

H

HEDGIE HEDGEHOG cake	54
HICKORY DICKORY DOCK cake	86
Hints and tips	23
HUMPTY DUMPTY cake	56

K

KING KONG cake	110

L

Lions	75
LUCKY HORSESHOE cake	100

M

Madeira Sponge	12
Male figure	27,51

N

(No.1) Indicates the use of a Mary Ford No.1 piping tube (see below). Other bracketed numbers indicate the appropriate tube number to be used.

NOAH'S ARK cake 92

O

ONE ARMED BANDIT cake 48

P

PESKY CROWS cake 50
Pigs 114
PLUMBER'S MATE cake 70
PORKY PIGLET cake 24
PUMPING IRON cake 44
PUSSYCATS cake 66

R

Recipes –
  All-in-one fruit cake 14
  All-in-one sponge 10
  All-in-one swiss roll 16
  Almond paste 18
  Butter icing 19
  Madeira sponge 12
  Modelling paste 19
  Royal icing 21
  Sugarpaste 20
Royal icing 21

RUCKSACK and BOOTS cake 84
RUGGER cake 29

S

SEWING BOX cake 77
SING-A-SONG OF SIXPENCE cake 106
Soldier 57
Sponge cake 10

Stippling: Royal icing should be stippled with a clean, dry household sponge or palette knife.

STRAWBERRIES and CREAM cake 52
Sugar 8
Sugarpaste 20
Swiss roll 16

T

THE MAD HATTER cake 38
THE MUMMY cake 36
THE THREE LITTLE PIGS cake 112
3 TODAY cake 60
TOYSHOP cake 34

U

U.F.O. cake 68

W

WEDDING TOPPERS cake 90
WINDMILL cake 64
Wolf 114

PIPING TUBES

The diagram shows the icing tube shapes used in this book. Please note that these are Mary Ford tubes, but comparable tubes may be used.

No.1   No.2   No.3   No.4   No.6

No.7   No.42   No.43   No.44   No.57

MARY FORD TITLES

101 Cake Designs
ISBN: 0 946429 55 3   320 pages
The original Mary Ford cake artistry text book. A classic in its field, over 200,000 copies sold.

Cake Making and Decorating
ISBN: 0 946429 41 3   96 pages
Mary Ford divulges all the skills and techniques cake decorators need to make and decorate a variety of cakes in every medium.

Jams, Chutneys and Pickles
ISBN: 0 946429 48 0   96 pages
Over 70 of Mary Ford's favourite recipes for delicious jams, jellies, pickles and chutneys with hints and tips for perfect results.

Kid's Cakes
ISBN: 0 946429 53 7   96 pages
33 exciting new Mary Ford designs and templates for children's cakes in a wide range of mediums.

Children's Birthday Cakes
ISBN: 0 946429 46 4   112 pages
The book to have next to you in the kitchen! Over forty new cake ideas for children's cakes with an introduction on cake making and baking to ensure the cake is both delicious as well as admired.

Party Cakes
ISBN: 0 946429 13 8   120 pages
36 superb party time sponge cake designs and templates for tots to teenagers. An invaluable prop for the party cake decorator.

Quick and Easy Cakes
ISBN: 0 946429 42 1   208 pages
The book for the busy mum. 99 new ideas for party and special occasion cakes.

Decorative Sugar Flowers for Cakes
ISBN: 0 946429 51 0   120 pages
33 of the highest quality handcrafted sugar flowers with cutter shapes, background information and appropriate uses.

Cake Recipes
ISBN: 0 946429 43 X   96 pages
Contains 60 of Mary's favourite cake recipes ranging from fruit cake to cinnamon crumble cake.

One Hundred Easy Cake Designs
ISBN: 0 946429 47 2   208 pages
Mary Ford has originated 100 cakes all of which have been selected for ease and speed of making. The ideal book for the busy parent or friend looking for inspiration for a special occasion cake.

Wedding Cakes
ISBN: 0 946429 39 1   96 pages
For most cake decorators, the wedding cake is the most complicated item they will produce. This book gives a full step-by-step description of the techniques required and includes over 20 new cake designs.

Home Baking with Chocolate
ISBN: 0 946429 37 5   96 pages
Over 60 tried and tested recipes for cakes, gateaux, biscuits, confectionery and desserts. The ideal book for busy mothers.

Making Cakes for Money
ISBN: 0 946429 44 8   120 pages
The complete guide to making and costing cakes for sale at stalls or to friends. Invaluable advice on costing ingredients and time accurately.

Biscuit Recipes
ISBN: 0 946429 50 2   96 pages
Nearly 80 home-bake sweet and savoury biscuit and tray bake recipes chosen for variety and ease of making.

The New Book of Cake Decorating
ISBN: 0 9462429 45 6   224 pages
The most comprehensive title in the Mary Ford list. It includes over 100 new cake designs and full descriptions of all the latest techniques.

A to Z of Cake Decorating
ISBN: 0 946429 52 9   208 pages
A guide to cake decorating, detailing traditional skills and the latest techniques. Over 70 new designs.

BOOKS BY MAIL ORDER

Mary Ford operates a mail order service in the U.K. for all her step-by-step titles. If you write to Mary at the address below she will provide you with a price list and details. In addition, all names on the list receive information on new books and special offers.

Write to: Mary Ford,
          30 Duncliff Road,
          Southbourne, Bournemouth,
          Dorset. BH6 4LJ. England.